D1379060

Salman Rushdie's Midnight's Children

Edited by
Reena Mitra

ATLANTIC
PUBLISHERS & DISTRIBUTORS (P) LTD

Published by

ATLANTIC
PUBLISHERS & DISTRIBUTORS (P) LTD

B-2, Vishal Enclave, Opp. Rajouri Garden,
New Delhi-110027
Phones : 25413460, 25429987, 25466842

Sales Office
7/22, Ansari Road, Darya Ganj,
New Delhi-110002
Phones : 23273880, 23275880, 23280451
Fax : 91-11-23285873
web : www.atlanticbooks.com
e-mail : info@atlanticbooks.com

Copyright © Atlantic Publishers and Distributors (P) Ltd., 2006

ISBN 81-269-0688-X

All rights reserved. No part of this publication may be
reproduced, stored in a retrieval system, transmitted or utilized
in any form or by any means, electronic, mechanical,
photocopying, recording or otherwise, without the prior
permission of the copyright owner. Application for such
permission should be addressed to the publisher.

Printed in India
at Nice Printing Press, Delhi

Preface

On its publication in 1980, Salman Rushdie's second novel, *Midnight's Children*, was internationally acclaimed as a literary masterpiece, the *piece de-resistance* that subsequently won the prestigious Booker McConnell Prize for fiction in 1981. Delicately poised between the artfully suggestive and the intriguingly subjective, the novel unerringly maintains the near perfect balance between fact and fiction. It is a highly imaginative and inspired commentary on life, life as lived in a specific period of the past, so that the novel truly becomes a mirror of the author's as well as the people's thoughts—these made articulate in the irresistible voice of a genius. The endeavour to unfold the enigma of the self and the effort to arrive at the facts of the times—"getting at the truth" as David Lodge says of Truman Capote's "new writing"—would both have proved abortive had Rushdie not, with his strikingly variant mode of portrayal, blended into a brilliant fabric autobiography and fictional narrative by distinctively fantasizing his depiction of history.

Rushdie's use of the fantastic as a mode of reality is witnessed in his very first novel, *Grimus*, through every aspect of which percolates to us remarkable inventiveness and a sense of the comic. His use of dream, myth and fantasy to reveal his particular kind of reality in which he sees the individual in relation to the larger historical forces that fashion the social structure around him is seen in the subsequent *Midnight's Children*, *Shame* as well as in the non-fictional *The Jaguar Smile*, which is a kind of travelogue based on the Nicaraguan situation of a society convalescing after the experience of a wave of violence and revolution, a situation parallel to the one in his own life. Later works, namely the controversial *Satanic Verses, Imaginary Homelands, Haroun and the Sea of Stories, The Moor's Last Sigh* and *The Ground Beneath Her Feet* are all ample proof of the fecundity of Rushdie's genius, but with *The Satanic Verses* and *The Moor's Last Sigh* the freshness and the originality of Rushdie's form of a blend of fact and fiction had, undoubtedly, started showing signs of enervation. *Fury,* Rushdie's next novel, though taken cognizance of, did not really stir the imagination of its readers but the literary world was still awaiting the publication of his new book which he had been "toodling away" at for two years as he himself tells us. That India would feature more prominently in it than in his earlier novel, *Fury,* which had been inspired by New York and every nuance of life there, was a piece of information that, again, was divulged to us by none other than the globally feted author himself.

Published in September, 2005 the four hundred page novel, *Shalimar the Clown,* was first released in its Portuguese version and then in English. The novel, flourishing an epic sweep characteristic of Rushdie, unfolds a passion play of love, betrayal, revenge and terror with the action being swirled from Kashmir to Strasbourg to Los Angeles. Some reviewers have clearly referred to this work as a book about terrorism but Rushdie himself has dismissed this categorization by saying that " the love story came first, as love stories should," but the "broken love that can't be fixed" is primarily an idiom for the fractured Kashmir, which "almost certainly can't be fixed." In *Shalimar the Clown,* Kashmir's terrorism-ridden landscape becomes the metaphor for the complete transformation of Rushdie's characters. Shalimar, for instance, transforms himself from clown to slayer for he learns early in life that metamorphosis is "a way of pushing back fate" and "choosing to remake the world." The creation of lithe and agile new selves has long been Rushdie's favourite preoccupation in his books. To put it simply, however, the novel follows the assassination of the American ambassador to Delhi, Maximilian Ophuls, his killer and his daughter. It is the story of a young Muslim boy who turns from a diffident teenager into an Islamic terrorist led by a radical mullah.

Today, the odious comparisons between Salman Rushdie and Vikram Seth that are entertained try to establish the superiority of the latter in terms of readability and universal appeal. There is, however, no justification for this because both have very different sensibilities and styles. Vikram Seth is a minimalist opting for multiple details while Rushdie wields sweeping canvases; Vikram maintains authorial distance in writing whereas Rushdie tends to be largely auto-biographical.

Despite the appearance of other writers on the firmament of Indian English writing, there is no gainsaying the fact that the credit for enabling the Indian English writer to come into his own goes largely to Rushdie. Popular Anglo-Indian authors like E.M. Forster and Ruth Prawer Jhabvala have now been replaced by a new breed of Indian novelists, biographers, political commentators and poets who, as Khushwant Singh admits "are much better than the old guard to which I belong. They handle the language a damn sight better."

It was Rushdie's *Midnight's Children* that made an indelible mark on the minds of its readers and pushed ajar the door that Rushdie himself had edged in through. He demonstrated that it was possible for Indians to write English in their own idiom and be considered seriously, to write English like the Indians and be accepted unconditionally. *Midnight's Children* was an unqualified success in its blending of history, myth and autobiography. The book operated at the level of fantasy but gained an amazing grasp of the cryptic and multi-layered reality of life in India. The comic in character, situation and language is effortlessly exploited providing, the novel with a strikingly fresh dimension. Rushdie, in *Midnight's Children*, devises what Kundera calls "a new art of novelistic counterpoint" and blends together philosophy, narrative and dream into one consummate whole.

REENA MITRA
Editor

Contents

1

Salman Rushdie's 'Midnight's Children': History and Fiction as Co-ordinates in Search for Meaning

REENA MITRA

Salman Rushdie, in *Midnight's Children*, shares with many other renowned novelists the choice of Indian history as a co-ordinate in his fictional art, the difference being that his presentation of historical facts covers a vaster span, from the pre-Independence Jallianwala Bagh incident of 1919 to the period of Emergency in 1977, and adopts a variant mode of portrayal. The facts themselves are of little interest as they have been repeatedly given to us by several novelists as well as historians. What is significant is how Rushdie has fantasized his depiction of historical reality. The introduction of the element of the magical and the supernatural has lent the work a dimension that makes it characteristically Rushdie's own, for he has his typical way of concocting a blend of art and life.

"Art," as Kakutani observes, "does have a way of imitating life, and writers have always been skeptical or incapable of unilaterally separating the two."[1] Salman Rushdie, too, in writing *Midnight's Children*, seems unable, by nature and by intention, to dissever the two. He had started, as Zola believed every literary artist did, "from the true facts, which are our indestructible basis," but to show "the mechanism of these facts,"[2] he had to modify them and it is in this specific orientation given to facts that his distinctive genius lies. By his own admission it is in *Midnight's Children* that he finds his "true voice."[3]

Nancy E. Batty, in her comparative study of the narrative techniques of *Midnight's Children* and *A Thousand and One Nights*,[4] draws careful attention to the dramatization of "the problematical relationship of life to art, art to life"[5] in *Midnight's Children*. This dramatization, she argues, is the effect of the deliberate juxtaposition of "the oriental tale, the eighteenth century Shandean novel and the modern historical 'realities' of India...."[6]

In an article in defence of his recent novel, *The Satanic Verses*, Rushdie has made his aesthetic predilections very clear when he says, "do not ask your writers to create 'typical' or 'representative' fictions. Such books are almost invariably dead books."[7] The novels that he really cares for are "those which attempt radical reformulations of language, form and ideas, those that attempt to do what the 'novel' seems to insist upon: to see the world anew."[8] And, this novel world view, if it provides implications that are worth thinking about, fulfils one of the important functions of literature.

Midnight's Children is a literary response to a series of real life situations that have been cleverly fictionalized through allusions, disguised as well as direct, to the country's recent as well as not so recent past. The novel has an epic sweep[9] covering about six decades in the history of the Indian subcontinent. Book One covers the time from the Jallianwala Bagh incident in April, 1919, to the birth of the protagonist, Saleem, on August 15, 1947; Book Two extends upto the end of the Indo-Pakistan war in September, 1965, and Book Three envelops the period upto the end of the Emergency in March, 1977, and includes the Bangladesh war as well.

At the fictional level, *Midnight's Children* depicts the events and experiences in the lives of three generations of the Sinai family. The account begins with their days in Srinagar and follows their passage through Amritsar, Agra and Bombay to Karachi, from where Saleem alone returns hidden in the basket of Parvati, the witch,[10] only to experience the tremors of the Emergency that had been clamped in India. At the semantic level, it is far more complex and has intriguing social and political connotations.

A careful analysis of *Midnight's Children* reveals three major aspects of Rushdie's use of history in his novel that deserve study: (i) the commingling of autobiography and narrative, (ii) the striking breach of chronology and (iii) the search for identity and the meaning of life, the quest for identity here being not merely that of the narrator-protagonist, Saleem Sinai, but also that of Padma, a persistent hint of whose self-assertiveness we are conscious of in the novel all through. The opening page of the novel gives us a decipherable clue to these features. Characteristically, Rushdie begins:

"I was born in the city of Bombay...once upon a time. No, that won't do, there's no getting away from the date: I was born in Dr. Narlikar's Nursing Home on August 15, 1947.[11] And the time?...On the stroke of midnight, as a matter of fact...at the precise instant of India's arrival at independence, I tumbled forth into the world! I had been mysteriously handcuffed to history, my destinies indissolubly chained to those of my country. For the next three decades, there was to be no escape.... I, Saleem Sinai, had become heavily embroiled in Fate—at the best of times, a dangerous sort of involvement.

Now, however, time (having no further use for me) is running out. I will soon be thirty-one years old! must work fast...if I am to end up meaning—yes, meaning—something.

And there are so many stories to tell, too many, such an excess of intertwined lives events miracles places rumours, so dense a commingling of the improbable and the mundane!.... I must commence the business of remaking my life from the point at which it really began, some thirty-two years before anything as obvious, as *present*, as my clock-ridden, crime-stained birth."[12]

The very first sentence of the work is illustrative of the hybrid art of the novelist. The tale is meant to be at once an autobiography and a narrative, an account of facts and a yarn spun out of imagination, a blend of truth and fiction. "I was born in the city of Bombay..." clearly sets the tone for an autobiography but the latter half of the sentence shifts the reader's attention and focus, and leaves him baffled as he makes a futile attempt to approximate fiction while facts call for their share of attention. He is mystified as to how "once upon a time" can be a natural sequel to what goes before. And yet, the two are confidently set against each other as a revelatory beginning to "so dense a commingling of the improbable and the mundane!"

That the novelist is not punctilious regarding the observance of chronology is also evident on the very first page of the book. There is a frequent forward or backward shift in time that makes it difficult to trace the proper sequence of events in the life of the protagonist. What the publisher's blurb[13] says of Rushdie's book *The Satanic Verses*, we can say of his *Midnight's Children*, too—"the past and the future chase each other furiously." At the very outset, after having given the date of his birth, the narrator somersaults to his thirty-first birthday. He then dives deep into the past only to return to the present, and then to embark upon the future. He feels that it is incumbent upon him "to write the future as I have written the past."[14]

This marked-break in chronology in the novel reveals the author's intention of giving not a record of events in the order of their occurrence but of projecting the basic historical truth as interacting with and affecting the life of the individual, that is, chiefly, the author himself as represented by the protagonist. On the one side we have Saleem's personal life, and, on the other, corresponding to this is the life and history of the nation. The story traces the various events in the life of the central character that synchronize with major happenings in the recent history of India. The parallel that is worked out, though strained at times, is designed to allow an understanding of the individual's life in terms of historical forces.

Also, one cannot but note that all through the novel Rushdie is preoccupied with a quest for identity and is impatient to gain an insight into the "meaning" of life. He has definitely launched out to search for the purpose of existence. "I must work faster," his protagonist tells us, "...if I am to end up meaning—yes meaning—something."[15] And again, "Am I so far gone in my desperate need for meaning, that I am prepared to distort everything?"[16] Later in the novel, there is a reference to "Saleem, with his desperation for meaning."[17] Such indicators in the narrative leave us in no doubt as to what the writer, consciously or unconsciously, has set out to accomplish in his work. And, if we are to take D.H. Lawrence's advice, we would, instead of trusting the artist, "trust the tale,"[18] and construe things in the light of whatever evidence there is in the work itself.

Returning, then, to the first of the significant aspects of the novel, there is no gainsaying the fact that Rushdie has ingeniously coupled the autobiographical with the fictional narrative. The narrator-protagonist, Saleem Sinai, prepares us at the very outset for just such a fusion when he writes of this "excess of intertwined lives events miracles places, rumours...."[19] The element of fantasy in the novel is introduced in such a matter-of-fact way that the reader swallows it almost unquestioningly, though he knows quite well that this is one of those extra-historical factors in the novel that lend it interest rather than authenticity. In fact, the juxtaposition of the two contrastive elements of fantasy[20] and reality[21] has been so skilfully effected in the narrative that one is left not with a sense of incongruity but with the consciousness of a comprehensive general design in which the magical and real shade off into each other very naturally, the former bringing into relief the historical truth the writer sets out to explore and fix.

Rushdie's protagonist talks about "the mind's divisions between fantasy and reality"[22] but in the novel itself no such divisions seem to exist for both these constituents jointly contribute towards the aesthetic realization of the author's as well as his narrator's "urge to encapsulate the whole of reality."[23] We have the symbolic *Lifafa Das*, the peep show man, who tries to capture "the whole of reality" in his box. Thus, the fantastic here is not merely "the occult, the inexplicable telepathy, people disappearing in baskets, and so on;"[24] it is essentially strategic in nature in the sense that it becomes a fictional mode of projecting reality and offers the real in terms of the fanciful and the bizarre.

Certain observations made in the course of the novel reveal Rushdie's attitude to reality, and bring home the message that the novelist's truth is different from that of the historian. "Sometimes legends make reality and become more useful than the facts,"[25] says Rushdie's narrator in trying to bring out the nature of fictional reality. And, again: "Reality can have metaphorical content; that does not make it less real."[26] It is clear that Rushdie's treatment of history is in conformity with his idea of "illusory fictional reality,"[27] which, while recording historical truth, does not insist upon a total transcription of reality.

Midnight's children themselves are metaphorically conceived in that they can be made to represent many things. The author himself suggests this:

> "They can be seen as the last throw of everything antiquated and retrogressive in our myth-ridden nation, whose defeat was entirely desirable in the context of a modernizing twentieth century economy; or as the true hope of freedom which is now forever extinguished; but what they must not become is the bizarre creation of a rambling diseased mind...."[28]

It is this "quality of visionary insights"[29] created by Rushdie's use of metaphors and symbols that lends distinction to his work.

Apart from the metaphorical value that the midnight's children have, each one of them has also been endowed with certain magical traits:

> "What made the events noteworthy was the nature of these children every one of whom was, through some freak of biology or perhaps owing to some preternatural power of the moment or just conceivably by sheer coincidence, endowed with features, talents and faculties which can only be described as miraculous."[30]

The supernatural qualities ascribed to these children are the author's means of lending validity to his protagonist's omniscience. Saleem's power of telepathy and the voices speaking inside his head enable him to provide the missing links in the narrative and to maintain the continuity of the story for "most of what matters in our lives takes place in our absence...."[31] Besides, even "memory cracks beyond hope of reassembly."[32] There are "fadings" and "gaps" and hence it is "necessary to improvise on occasion"[33]—"the trick is to fill in the gaps."[34]

The providing of miraculous powers to the children born on the midnight of Independence also enables the novelist to expatiate upon the superhuman traits of the mythic Hindu heroes by comparing his "midnight's children" with these prodigies:

"So among the Midnight's Children were infants with powers of transmutation, flight, prophecy and wizardry... but two of us were born on the stroke of midnight. Saleem and Shiva...to Shiva the hour had given the gifts of war (of Ram who could draw the undrawable bow; of Arjuna and Bhima, the ancient prowess of Kurus and Pandavas united unstoppably in him !)...."[35]

Saleem himself refers to his "miraculous nature, which involved me beyond all mitigation in the myth life of India."[36]

Rushdie's sense of fantasy seen in his prolific inventiveness[37] and comic approach pervades his entire art of novel writing but it is never allowed to exist without the surer base of realism which lends the world of the book a truth of its own. It is his "bivision of fact and fantasy"[38] then, that strikes the balance. Rushdie's defence of his use of fantasy in *The Satanic Verses* is equally applicable to *Midnight's Children*: "I genuinely believed that my overt use of fabulation would make it clear to any reader that I was not attempting to falsify history, but to allow a fiction to take off from history...."[39] Elsewhere in the same article, Rushdie explains: "Fiction uses facts as the starting place and then spirals away to explore its real concerns, which are only tangentially historical...."[40]

In *Midnight's Children* Rushdie has ingeniously demonstrated his ability to historify myth and fictionalize history. His most potent message in the novel, as Nancy E. Batty points out, is that "if history is composed of fictions, then fiction can be composed of history."[41] In this regard it is noteworthy that in *Midnight's Children* the degree of fantasy introduced varies with the extent of his acquaintance with facts. He indulges in fantasy when he is ignorant or unsure of facts to fill in the "gaps", as the narrator tells us. His Pakistan is more of a fantasy[42] than reality and he himself admits it with characteristic casualness: "Anyway, it was not 'my' country...,"[43] he makes his protagonist in the novel say. It is, however, not true that he did not know enough about Pakistan, for he does give us in a nutshell a fairly authentic history of that nation and he also tries to establish "connections" with that country; for example, we hear Saleem say, "I helped to change the fate of the land of the Pure"[44] and "...with the Fate of the nation in my hand."[45] But, he certainly knew much more about India, the country of his birth, and, at certain unguarded moments, his emotional ties clearly reveal themselves. In one of his interviews, Rushdie tells us about *Midnight's Children*:

> "Well, I suppose, it began by being a novel of memory. The original motivation was to write about my childhood home, Bombay, at the time when I was growing up there...."[46]

This original motivation, however, took on larger implications and the work came to be a literary exploration of "the memory of a society in political and social decline."[47]

Rushdie's blending of fiction and fact we see also in the especial way in which he portrays imaginary people—though some of his characters are clearly identifiable—reacting to real events. The result again is the desired one: a kind of mythicized history, a work that conveys more the feeling than the facts of the period, though the basic limits imposed by history are never entirely violated.

The "real" events that Rushdie depicts are not mere concrete incidents tracing the political history of India from the pre-Independence days to the present times; they comprise the complex of events and situations that is certainly not quantifiable.[48] *Midnight's Children* does not reveal the movement of history in vividly realized concrete occurrences given in their chronological order, nor does it depend on meticulous details. In fact, as we have already seen, there is a marked-break in chronology and this is significant in revealing the novelist's intention and design. The novel is not meant to be a bald chronological account of the period portrayed. It concentrates on projecting the kind of fuller historical truth that incorporates the social and historical reality of the times as interacting with, and affecting, the life of the individual, that is, chiefly the protagonist himself who undoubtedly represents the author.

On the other hand, the imaginary characters portrayed are indicative of the novelist's indulgence in fantasy and imagination. All the "Midnight's Children" have been endowed with certain magical powers and it is through them that we learn to accept the fantastic in the novel. The other characters, too, range from the absolutely human to the strikingly superhuman, from man in general to witches and wizards. Interestingly, while Rushdie's men are not without the power to crystallize the drops of blood coming out of their nostrils into rubies, the inmates of the magicians' ghetto are not devoid of human feelings and sentiments.

So, Rushdie in *Midnight's Children* has made of history "an amazing pot-pourri of clever tricks."[49] He has framed his own "literary aesthetic of truth telling"[50] which skilfully incorporates factual as well as experiential truth.[51] He has availed himself of the artist's license to take certain imaginative liberties in his work with the intention of giving narrative shape to recorded facts. He re-enacts the past in terms of recognizable constructs and configurations and in doing so, he "allows himself the freedom to weed out pure facts or events, to twist facts, as long as the final view of history does not contradict what happened in the larger scheme."[52]

Rushdie, clearly represented by Saleem, the narrator of his novel, makes of his childhood memories a powerful creative force[53] and in writing about his own life and that of his nation, he chooses the vantage point of the present and his mind delves deep into the past giving the tale a historical perspective.

Waghmare, in assessing Chinua Achebe's vision of the past, discusses the novelist's assumption of the part of a biographer:

"When a novelist deals with the past of his own people or community, he has to assume the role of a biographer. A biographer, as André Maurois points out, has two duties: he must be a portrait painter and a historian (Maurois, 1960: 39). As an historian he should discover the cultural heritage of his people and chronicle all the important events that might have changed the destiny and moulded the social pattern of his people.... Soon he realizes that the past of his people or community is his own past in a way...."[54]

Rushdie, too, in chronicling his own past and that of his people, takes on the mantle of a biographer and performs his "duties" effectively, that is, the duty of a portrait painter as well as that of an historian. The work, however, becomes easier when he reminds himself of the parallel drawn by Henry James between the art of the painter and that of the novelist "as the picture is reality, so the novel is history."[55] It is not enough to offer the reader a mere journalistic reproduction. As Howell puts its, "when realism becomes false to itself, when it heaps up facts merely, and maps life instead of picturing it, realism will perish, too."[56] Rushdie is well aware of this aspect of the art of the novelist as historian. He avoids piling up facts and making his work only a mirror of the times. His is not a mere conventional chronological narration of history but there certainly is a forward linear movement in the account that traces the history of the protagonist and his "twin," the nation, from the pre-Independence days, through the attainment of Independence to the recent times. The telescoping of time and the condensation of space is noteworthy. Also, the novel certainly does have an irreversible linear progression which K. Raghavendra Rao fails to identify. When Rao ventures to say, "Indeed the novel can be read backward without any essential loss of direction or location,"[57] obviously, he has failed to appreciate the informing principle underlying the narrative structure. Besides, history, irrespective of how much of it is given to us through the novel, can never be traced backward, for it is characterized by an irreversible forward movement. Linked to history, the growth of the protagonist as well as that of the nation is seen as a process. There is no going back.

That the novel is autobiographical in content is evident from what Salman-Saleem says in the course of the story-telling... "I reach the end of my long-winded autobiography; in words and pickles, I have immortalized my memories."[58] Saleem, at the time of narration, is working in a pickle factory and in writing this saga hopes that:

"...one day, perhaps, the world may taste the pickles of history. They may be too strong for some palates, their smell may be overpowering, tears may rise to the eyes; I hope nevertheless that it will be possible to say of them that they possess the authentic taste of truth."[59]

He clarifies his stand further and warns us against unsuspecting faith in his version of factuality—"distortions are inevitable in both methods (i.e. words and pickles). We must live, I am afraid, with the shadows of imperfection."[60] Somewhere he writes, "I remain conscious that errors have already been made..., the risk of unreliability grows"[61] but "in autobiography, as in all literature, what actually happened is less important than what the author can manage to persuade his audience to believe...."[62] So, autobiography is not totally reliable, authentic history, yet it is made convincing by a parallel narration of the biagraphy of the members of Saleem's family and of the concomitant reconstruction of the history of the nation. Saleem himself refers to the probability of his being "only the first historian to write the story of my undeniably exceptional life and times."[63]

Regarding the break in chronology in *Midnight's Children* it is evident from the very beginning that the author never had in mind a sustained biographical account of the life of the protagonist or a record of historical events in order of time. As he himself tells us, his purpose in writing the novel was to focus on "the connection between public affairs and private lives." As he elaborates, "You cannot separate the two. They interpenetrate and that is how the writer needs to examine them, the one in the context of the other."[64] It is with this objective of examining "one in the context of the other" in view that Rushdie concentrates on the junctural events in the life of Saleem as well as that of the nation. In the novel, on the one side we have Saleem's personal life, and on the other, corresponding to this is the life of the nation. Yet, in the lives of both, only those events which demonstrate the interaction of the two have been selected. The story traces the various crises in the life of the protagonist that synchronize with the major events and movements in the history of modern India the Jallianwala Bagh tragedy, the Quit India Movement, the Cabinet Mission, the struggle for Independence, the role of the Muslim League, the post-Independence riots, the Five-Year Plans, the re-organization of the states in India, the language agitation, the Chinese aggression, the theft of the sacred relic from Hazratbal mosque, the war with Pakistan, the Independence of Bangladesh, the Emergency and other historical landmarks. This varied experience, including the ordeal of the freedom movement, became, as Shyam M. Asnani puts it, "a part of the life of almost all the sensitive and enlightened Indians."[65]

Saleem, from the very beginning, as he himself tells us, is conscious of his "centrality" in giving direction to the major events in the history of the nation. At one point in time, much later in life, he even considers himself a "competitor for centrality"[66] along with Indira Gandhi, who was perhaps unaware of the role of the mirror-of-the-nation bestowed on Saleem by her father, Jawahar Lal Nehru, in his letter to Baby Saleem.[67] In fact, in the novel, Saleem's life is the microcosm that reflects and affects the macrocosmic life of the state and reverberates with the impact of the happenings that plague the latter. Saleem is born at midnight on August 15, 1947, the very moment at which India attained her Independence. He is one of the thousand and one midnight's children who are also "the children of the time; fathered...by history."[68] The child and the nation go through parallel experiences of the pangs of birth, the caprices of childhood, the traumas of adolescence and the uncertainties of adulthood. As a consequence of the coincidence of his birth and the consistency of this synchrony between his life and the nation's, Saleem becomes "heavily embroiled in Fate"[69] and is "mysteriously handcuffed to history,"[70] his destinies "indissolubly chained"[71] to those of his country. He is conscious throughout, of his "historical role,"[72] for on his shoulders is placed the mantle of being "the newest bearer of that ancient face of India which is also eternally young"[73] and of mirroring the life of the nation. But his historical role does not merely mark him out as the recipient of the impact of historical events; his own personal realities in life often direct the course of history:[74] "Already my very presence is having an effect on history; already Baby Saleem is working changes on people around him...."[75] And, this continues consistently enough to make one acquiesce in Saleem's observation at the close of the novel: "...it is the privilege and the curse of midnight's children to be both masters and victims of their times."[76]

At a critical time in the history of the "child-nation"[77] when Five-Year Plans are being charted and elections are in the offing, when language marchers are vociferously demanding the division of Bombay according to linguistic boundaries, the nine-year old Saleem acquires the miraculous gift of telepathy by which he can enter into the minds of people, "tune"[78] his inner ear to their inside-voices to learn their secrets.

This "eavesdropping"[79] on people he knew is Saleem's first entry into the public affairs of India:

> "I paradoxically took my first tentative steps towards that involvement with mighty events and public lives from which I would never again be free...never, until the Widow...."[80]

And, henceforth, every event in Saleem's life is linked with some incident in the life of the nation. The elections of 1957 take place before his tenth birthday. A little after his eleventh birthday, "at the end of the year of accelerated history,"[81] Saleem attains his full adult height and then, in the elections of 1962, just as 'status quo' is maintained in India so nothing changes in Saleem's life, too. On Dec. 16, 1971, when Saleem, after his period of exile in Pakistan, returns to India concealed in Parvati's wicker-basket, Mrs. Gandhi is celebrating her fresh lease of life in Indian politics, for her new Congress party now holds more-than-two-thirds majority in the National Assembly. In a fit of rage, Saleem resolves to give the nation as he had given himself, the right to choose a better future for he looks upon the country as "not only my twin-in-birth but also joined to me (so to speak) at the hip, so that what happened to either of us, happened to us both."[82]

At this juncture in the life of both, Saleem and the nation, the pace of history accelerates and there are a number of synchronous events on either side. Shiva's "explosion"[83] into the life of Saleem at the magicians' ghetto coincides with India's surprising nuclear capability demonstrated with the first nuclear explosions in the deserts of Rajasthan on 18th May 1974. The wedding celebrations of Saleem and Parvati synchronize with the Republic Day festivities in the country and from then onward the parallels drawn between the life of the protagonist and that of the nation continue through Parvati alias Laylah Sinai; at the time that Laylah enters labour, Indira Gandhi is found guilty of malpractices in the previous elections; Laylah's son, Aadam Sinai, is born on 15th June 1975, the day the Emergency was imposed in India; he, too, like Saleem is "mysteriously handcuffed to history,"[84] and his fortunes are inseparably linked with those of his country; his distress caused by tuberculosis is suspected of having "something darkly metaphorical"[85] in it; it seems to be a manifestation of his "connection-to-history:"[86]

> "...believing that, in those midnight months when the age of my connection-to-history overlapped with his, our private emergency was not unconnected with the larger macrocosmic disease; under whose influence the sun had become as pallid and diseased as our son."[87]

And then, history "narrowed down to this final full point!"[88] Saleem is arrested and imprisoned, he loses his freedom and (significantly enough he loses with it his silver spittoon swallowed by bulldozers to sever him from "the last object connecting me to my more tangible, historically verifiable past."[89] Saleem is given no reason for his incarceration, for "Who of all the thirty thousand or quarter of a million was told why or wherefore? who needed to be told?"[90] The culmination, however, comes with Saleem's forced sterilization so that now he is "no longer connected to history, drained above and drained below."[91] Irrevocable harm has been done but, finally, appeasement comes with the fall of the Widow with which also vanished the ailment of Aadam Sinai.

The consistent equation drawn between the principal character in the novel and the nation is a measure to make explicit the empathy experienced by the former (and his creator) with his "twin-in-birth."[92] This is how Rushdie projects his concept of history as interacting with the individual and we are introduced to his idea of the interplay of the two on the very first page. Rushdie himself declares that everything in his two novels, *Midnight's Children* and *Shame*, "has had to do with poetics and with the relationship of the individual and history."[93] In particular, Book Three of *Midnight's Children*, he feels, has "more to do with the direct collision of the individual with history;"[94] it deals with the Emergency and its consequences. History in the novel is mediated through the narrator's consciousness and hence the apology for whatever distortions there may be. Born of history, the narrator gives birth (as creator) to history and this reciprocal creative activity knows no end till he is "sucked into the annihilating whirlpool of the multitudes,"[95] and ceases to exist as an individual. Rushdie creates in his protagonist a chronicler who registers in his life the interplay of the public and the private spheres. Keith Wilson refers to Saleem as "a narrator who, quite literally, is the history that he records," and, elaborating further, he says: "He subsumes most matter of public record within himself."[96]

Rushdie's vision is clearly historical rather than personal in the sense that he is inclined to see the individual in relation to the larger social and historical forces that condition his life. In *Midnight's Children*, Rushdie's purpose, as B.K. Joshi points out, is "to relate private lives to public events and to explore the limits of individuality in a country as big, as populous and culturally variegated as India."[97] Rushdie is temperamentally averse to brooding. He does not withdraw inwards for his unhappy meditations. He avoids solipsistic reflections. His is not the imagination of escape, but of confrontation. He would rather grapple with intransigent reality and expose it than buy his peace by shutting his eyes to it. Consequently, some of this tendency rubs off on his characters, chiefly his protagonist. This results in an interesting insight which is revealed in Rushdie's realization that while great events take place around human beings, the truly significant developments occur within them, and that to understand life in its totality, one must recognize their inter-relatedness. Just as the powerful tide of history cannot be stemmed by an individual, so too the latter's will or vision cannot be entirely paralyzed by history and his personal life is of interest in itself. It is this belief that makes Rushdie observe that "the small individual lives of men are preferable to all this inflated macrocosmic activity."[98]

Rushdie has, perhaps, carried this parallel between the life of the protagonist with the life of the nation a little too far, but then the matrix of events embroiling both the individual and the state has been so designed as to allow an understanding of the individual primarily in terms of the historical forces that operate in his life.[99] In his efforts to discover the "modes-of-connection," the writer may have stretched his imagination to excess but we may forgive him this as his attempt at understanding the history of the nation is only a strategy for a comprehension of the self.[100] He declares: "I am what I am only in relation to those about me," and his "those" together comprise "the other"[101] in relation to whom we see ourselves. One can have a sense of continuity on the wide map of history which is not easy to perceive in one's life because a nation's history encompasses far more space and time and can be studied on a much larger-scale than an individual's. Moreover, the far greater range of history and its multiple perspectives afford a more complete understanding of the challenges an individual has to face and his capabilities to cope with them.

There is yet another advantage of implicating history in one's fate. As we know, proximity to an event tends to cause a loss of perspective. So Rushdie's use of history in an attempt to understand his own life may be seen as an appropriate distancing device. As he explains in the novel:

> "Reality is a question of perspective; the further you get from the past, the more concrete and plausible it seems— but as you approach the present, it inevitably seems more and more incredible."[102]

And when we are too close to what is happening, "...perspective is impossible...we're too close to the cinema screen, the picture is breaking up into dots." So, in the absence of a proper perspective "only subjective judgements are possible."[103] One delves into the past, therefore, to understand the present in terms of the by-gones and through indirections to find directions.

It needs to be admitted that even when the past is evoked, it is punctuated by intermittent references to the present to remind us where we are in point of time and to maintain the proper perspective. Padma's presence as "narratee" and as Saleem's "necessary ear"[104] in any recountal of the past is indication enough of the point of view of the narrator. This point of view undergoes several shifts in the course of the novel. Chronology thus remains sacrificed to perspective.

Rushdie's treatment of history is probably a matter of scale. This may have decided his choice of setting one up against the other the narrowly individual against the broadly public. Besides, the consistent parallel drawn between the individual and the subcontinent is also a deliberate aesthetic choice that helps the writer set the parameters of the plot structure of the novel and give it form. Form is important; nay, inevitable. As Rushdie observes: "Everything has a shape if you look for it. There is no escape from form."[105]

Walter Allen speaks of contemporary novels as "the mirror of the age," a special kind of mirror reflecting "not merely the external features of the age but also its innerface, its nervous system, coursing of its blood and the unconscious prompting and conflicts which sway it."[106] *Midnight's Children* too, is a mirror reflecting, "the deeper stirrings"[107] of the life of the times. Saleem's life, which is the novel, is sketched in metaphoric relation to the life of the nation. Aroused into analysis by the contents of the Prime Minister's letter, written to him at the time of his birth "Your life will be, in a sense, the mirror of our own"[108] Saleem is set thinking as to "How, in what terms, may the career of a single individual be said to impinge on the fate of a nation?"[109] And then, after strained thought comes the enlightenment, and the "modes-of-connection"[110] are established:

> "I must answer in adverbs and hyphens: I was linked to history both literally and metaphorically, both actively and passively, in what our (admirably modern) scientists might term 'modes-of-connection' composed of dualistically combined configurations of the two pairs of opposed adverbs given above. This is why hyphens are necessary: actively-literally, passively-metaphorically, actively-metaphorically and passively-literally, I was inextricably entwined with my world."[111]

Saleem explains further: "By the combination of 'active' and 'literal' I mean, of course, all actions of mine which directly literally–affected, or altered the course of seminal historical events."[112] And, he goes on to relate how he provided the language marchers demanding the creation of the linguistic states of Gujarat and Maharashtra with their battle cry and thus became actively involved in public events. The second 'mode' "the union of 'passive' and 'metaphorical'"[113] included all socio-political trends and events which merely by their existence affected Saleem metaphorically, for example, in the reference to "The Fisherman's Pointing Finger" lay the latent connection between the child-nation's efforts to acquire adulthood and Saleem's own gigantic attempts at growing up. Here, the public affected the private in a rather extensive manner. The third 'mode-of-connection'—the 'active-metaphorical'—encompassed all those occasions on which "things done by or to me were mirrored in the macrocosm of public affairs"[114] and Saleem's individual existence was symbolical of the nation's state. The mutilation of Saleem's little finger had let out spurts of blood; history, too, was marked by a similar maiming and bloody violence had erupted. Lastly, the 'passive-literal' covered all moments at which "national events had a direct bearing upon the lives of myself and my family."[115] Saleem includes under this head the freezing of his father's property and the explosion at Walkeshwar Reservoir.

The various 'modes-of-connection' established between the protagonist and the nation clearly demonstrate the individual's shaping of history and, in turn, being shaped by it.

This correspondence, though drawn too far, enables the novelist to blend the autobiographical, biographical and historical into an organic narrative, which carries with it not only credibility and the "solidity of specification"[116] but also a sharpened consciousness of reality that convincingly relates the past to the present and "involves a perception, not only of the past, but of its presence."[117]

Metaphors in *Midnight's Children*, if rightly interpreted, often provide a key to an understanding of the novel and the reality it projects. A prominent and sustained metaphor in the work used in relation to the similar lives of Saleem and the nation is that of the "chutnification of history"[118] the pickling of time. The symbolic significance of the pickling process is that it preserves time and experience private as well as public and makes them available to the generations to come. The taste of the pickles may be "too strong" for some and their smell "overpowering"[119] for others, but they do, hopefully, preserve the taste of truth.

The requirements for "chutnification" are obviously raw materials—fruits, vegetables, fish, vinegar, spices. But also clear, penetrating eyes which can gauge the true quality of the vegetables, and a "discerning"[120] nose that can decide "what-must-be-pickled, its humours and messages and emotions...."[121] At Braganza Pickles are prepared not only Mary's recipes but also "Saleem's special blends"[122] which include "memories, dreams, ideas"[123] and which are for mass-consumption: "Thirty jars stand upon a shelf, waiting to be unleashed upon the amnesiac nation."[124] In other words, the past is re-interpreted and articulated for those who wish to taste "the pickles' version of history:"[125]

"There are, of course, because of 'the spice bases' the inevitable distortions of the pickling process. To pickle is to give immortality, after all..., a certain alteration, a slight intensification of taste, is a small matter, surely? The art is to change the flavour in degree, but not in kind; and above all...to give it shape and form—that is to say, meaning."[126]

This is Rushdies's aesthetic credo expressed in an easily understandable domestic image. The externals are of no consequence; what matters is the spirit of the thing.

Saleem refers to his tale as "memory's truth,"[127] and what differentiates this truth from any other kind of truth is that:

"memory has its own special kind. It selects, eliminates, alters, exaggerates, minimizes, glorifies, and vilifies also; but in the end it creates its own reality, its heterogeneous but usually coherent version of events; and no sane human being ever trusts someone else's version more than his own."[128]

"Memory's truth" is highly selective and sets the limits of its own reality.

Rushdie's "chutnification" may be seen as an attempt to blend and mix ideas and events, individual life and public life in such a way as to give life a sense of continuity in the future that he has a longing for, and that he probably feared as lost on the memorable midnight. This explains his reference to his son and his son's son carrying on the process begun by him. We normally look back for a sense of continuity but he has brought the past into the present in order to extend his desire for a sense of continuity into the future. For him, the past is not over but continues to make itself felt through its impact. So, it becomes a function of his life in the present. No wonder the boundaries are blurred not only between past and present but also between fact and fiction, imagination and reality.

Rushdie dreams his desire into reality, the reality which consists of his life and his country's. The desire for immortality as well as that for continuity are parallel desires, both of which Rushdie cherishes and expresses forcefully.[129]

Another important metaphor in the novel is that of the perforated cloth through which Saleem's grandfather, Dr. Aadam Aziz, once examined as a patient his grandmother Naseem before he married her. The implication is that narrative is a perforated sheet which conceals the whole, revealing only parts which appear in the nature of "trailers"[130] to arouse our curiosity. We come now to the third major aspect of the use of history in the novel, viz. the search for identity. *Midnight's Children*, like *The Satanic Verses*, is written from "the experience of uprooting"[131] that comes from the migrant condition. Rushdie himself, in an interview by the B.B.C. refers to the "aspects of personal history"[132] contained in *Midnight's Children*. "A man from too many places"[133] he calls himself. Born in India and living in Britain, he is "a product of biethnicity,"[134] which according to Suryanarayana Murti is "the creative matrix of his fiction."[135]

Dr. Alistair Niven, referring to Rushdie and all those Indian writers, who live in England but write about their own subcontinent, describes what they would term "detachment" in their works as "a deracinated loss of identity..."[136] "...it is hard to see where they belong."[137] says he. Rushdie himself confirms this "sense of deracination"[138] experienced by him while studying at Rugby School, where racial prejudice was so pronounced that for the first time he realized that he belonged to "a race" and "suddenly in England I became Indian."[139] The irony, however, lay in the fact that while in England he felt like an alien, in India his family felt discriminated against and moved to Pakistan. But even that move failed. So, when he settled down in England, he began to reach for his roots, and *Midnight's Children* became the medium of the quest of one who could never really "belong" anywhere.

Ashutosh Banerjee refers to Saleem in *Midnight's Children* as "Rushdie's fictional alter ego"[140] Saleem, having been born at the precise moment at which India attained her Independence, establishes a kinship with his creator in that the latter, too, was born about that time, that is, two months before the Indian Independence, in June 1947, in Bombay. Rushdie has deliberately fictionalized his date of birth in his novel for narrative purposes, for it is the time of Saleem's birth that subjects him to a more difficult fate by giving his identity a larger dimension. It is as "midnight's child" born on 15 August 1947, that Saleem, is "mysteriously handcuffed to history."[141] He becomes, as M.K. Naik observes, conscious of his "larger identity"[142] rather early in life. Naik draws attention to "the protagonist's identity crisis"[143] and comes to the conclusion that *Midnight's Children*:

> "illustrates the permanent plight of individual identity in the hostile modern world which makes it impossible for anyone to remain an island but compels everyone to be part of a continent, with the result that the individual is inevitably 'handcuffed to history.'"[144]

Thus, the central theme of the novel, according to Naik, is the fate of individual identity in a hostile world, which causes it to suffer fragmentation and sterility and re-establishing one's identity with others and communicating with them alone make one's bid for definition a valid one and the resistance one encounters in it may be a test of strength—or even a promise of it.

Saleem is the central consciousness in the novel, whose ordeals and tribulations are closely followed and analyzed. He is an extremely sensitive and self-conscious narrator (like his creator), and, in spite of all other weaknesses, is confident of his competence as a story-teller. He knows that Padma, who, as Nancy Batty points out, is the "index for reader-response to the framed narrative,"[145] will not be able to resist the charm of his narration: "No doubt about it: my story has her by the throat."[146] Padma as narratee does offer attention in exchange for information but, seems well aware of the "constructedness"[147] of Saleem's narration, for she can seldom comprehend any connection between Saleem's stories and his "real" existence. "...there is reason to believe," says Nancy Batty, "that even Saleem's explicit audience, Padma, regards

Saleem's autobiography as a fiction."[148] Thus Saleem, like his maker, is a "creator rather than recorder of his own history."[149] and suggests that by "filling in the gaps where...memory cracks,"[150] he presents a narrative, that is, in the ultimate analysis, tentative rather than unalterable and final—tentative because it deals in "broken mirrors, some of whose fragments have been irretrievably lost."[151]

Despite the tentative nature of the narrative that Saleem weaves out of his fractured human perception he never, during the course of the narrative, abandons his pursuit of the meaning of life, though "meaning he knows (as his creator does) is a shaky edifice that we build out of scraps, dogmas, childhood injuries, newspaper articles, chance remarks, people you love, people you hate, old films, small victories."[152]

Saleem is conscious of the whirling speed with which time is passing and in his search for identity and "meaning", he races against time which is "running out."[153] He never gives up the quest for meaning, though he has to maintain all along a certain degree of caution, for, in his desire to place himself in a central role, he is inclined to misrepresent things; this apprehension is revealed in his self-analysis later:

> "Am I so far gone in my desperate need for meaning, that I'm prepared to distort everything—to rewrite the whole history of my times purely in order to place myself in its central role? Today, in my confusion I can't judge. I'll have to leave it to others...."[154]

But soon, "after years of yearning for importance,"[155] Saleem, the buddha, who had abandoned consciousness and deliberately severed himself from history, comes to the realization that any determination to espouse a historical role was futile for every individual is nothing but a drop in the river of human life, and yet, human life is what it is merely because of the presence of that one drop and many other such drops:

> "Who, what am I? My answer: I am the sum total of everything that went before me, of all I have been seen done, of everything done to me. I am everyone, everything of whose being-in-the-world affected was affected by

mine. I am anything that happens after I have gone which would not have happened if I had not come. Nor am I particularly exceptional in this matter; each 'I', everyone of the now-six-hundred-million-plus of us, contains a similar multitude. I report for the last time, to understand me, you will have to swallow a world."[156]

Thus, each individual can claim an identity of his own, and yet, he has to submit to a final merger with the milling myriads who make their respective contributions and then pass into anonymity.

Saleem, like his creator, believes firmly in the ultimate merging in of the individual with the multitudes so that he is no longer a separate entity but an inseparable part of the "many." This faith is harboured with unflagging conviction from the first to the last page of the novel. In the beginning, Saleem tells us:

"I have been a swallower of lives; and to know me just the one of me, you'll have to swallow the lot as well. Consumed multitudes are jostling and shoving inside me;
...."[157]

At the end, too, his faith remains unchanged and he reaffirms his belief: "...I have been so-many too-many persons."[158] And he visualizes himself being "sucked into the annihilating whirlpool of the multitudes."[159]

Attributing Rushdie's protagonist's problems of identity to the writer himself, one would be inclined to think that throughout the novel Rushdie is pre-occupied with a search for identity.[160] There is, I feel, justification enough for this though Rushdie himself would have us believe that he is engaged in no such quest:" I know who I am and I don't have a sense of having an identity crisis. But people keep telling me I should."[161]

But, an assertion is no proof. Any writer of consequence, though professedly objective in his depiction of life and reality, is only relatively so, for the self in the artist in irrepressible and insidiously winds its way through into the creation. A writer, then, is simultaneously, objective and subjective, and is involved in a somewhat paradoxical exercise: an intellectually creative balancing act in which invention and creativity which are largely subjective and judgement which is essentially expected to be objective, co-ordinate to achieve and preserve equilibrium in his endeavour to make sense of experience. All art, in the ultimate analysis, is an expression of man's urge for self-creation. Thus we cannot always take the writer's word as the ultimate authority to arrive at our conclusions, for he may be either deliberately misleading us in our attempt at interpretation, or he may himself be unconsciously trying to establish his identity. This will become clear presently. Such close parallels and correspondences between the life of the protagonist and that of the nation can be drawn only by one who himself is deeply involved, and thus finds it difficult to maintain objectivity and distance in his art[162] in spite of every distancing device adopted. Saleem clearly filters for us the author's own experiences.

The central query in *Midnight's Children*, then, is: what is the compulsion aesthetic or personal that makes the novelist assiduously weave such a complex web of parallels between the life of the protagonist (who may very well be identified with the novelist himself) and, that of the nation? Could it be the artist's own way of reconstructing meaning out of the chaos of the times, of discovering his identity in the context of a large perspective? In spite of the novelist's denial one has little doubt that the work is a verbalization of the writer's quest for identity, his desire to "belong" somewhere and to discover where he belongs; an expression of his urge to know how he came to be what he is and how he came to be where he is. To Keats, "what the imagination seizes as beauty must be the truth;" to Rushdie, what the fancy apprehends as content must be the meaningful truth. The apparently fanciful images and constructs must merge into a significant whole. Thus, what Rushdie embarks upon is an exploration of his life, which he identifies with the life of the state, and more specifically, with the life of the particular community to which he belongs, viz. the Indian Muslims, the world 'Indian' here having greater import and significance for him than the latter word for he has always been full of what he calls "Bombayness" in *Midnight's Children* and "the India-idea" elsewhere. Multiplicity, plurality, incompatible realities and different faiths—this is what modern India is all about and Rushdie is very much a product of it—what he needs is reassurance and understanding and a re-acquaintance with Bombay, his "lost city."[163]

One admires in Rushdie, as one does in Dickens, the intellectual audacity to adopt fantasy as a means of depicting truth, for verisimilitude[164] and historical precision alone do not seem to serve his desire to project the kind of reality he wishes to. Fantasy allows a free play to the mind that realism would restrain, and hence a balance has to be struck between the fantastic and the real, for "this elusive and profound relationship between history and private fantasy is repeatedly the key to a whole fictional world."[165]

Rushdie's fantasizing mixed with first-person narrative, is a kind of modernistic device to stress the fictive nature of his fiction as also to accommodate fantasy to fact to represent or re-enact better those aspects of reality that have been poignantly experienced by him and would not be easily captured in words which never fail in a realistic novel. Rushdie, a man of varied sensibility, caught between the cross-currents of the individual and the historical, the personal and the national, and, what Yeats in his poem, "Under Ben Bulben" calls "the two eternities of soul and race," set the trend for autobiographical writing in modern Indian English fiction with his *Midnight's Children* which won him the Booker Prize in 1981. The novel, however, as pointed out before, is an autobiographical work with a difference—it offers a peculiar blend of the factual and the fantastic which characterizes the microcosmic reality of the novel and provides for the varied nuances and contours of individual experience. It demonstrates the author's firm conviction that "it is entirely possible for a novel to be autobiographical and also to be completely fictional. That's what my book is,"[166] says Rushdie. Rushdie undoubtedly found his voice with *Midnight's Children* and the world of the book has a truth of its own, a truth with which he is armed to deal seriously with life as he sees it.

As Tom Wolfe asserts, "fantasy is a part of reality,"[167] but for Rushdie, it is so much more; it helps him rise above reality and "assert a seeming independence of creativity as the distinctive quality of art."[168] It not only stresses the fictive element in the narrative but is, indeed, revelatory of the mind behind the work. In other words, it is self-reflexive fiction in which fiction is nothing but a mode of reality, the reality of the author's self-caught in a complex interplay with historical reality.

Fantasy in *Midnight's Children*, besides being a form of reality, also serves to add spice to the narrative and to provide relief from the strain of trying to comprehend the truth in terms of the factual. It energetically exploits the comic in character, situation and language providing the novel a strikingly fresh and absorbing dimension. Rushdie, in *Midnight's Children*, devises what Kundera visualizes as "a new art of novelistic counter-point (which can blend philosophy, narrative and dream into one music);...."[169]

REFERENCES

1. Michiko Kakutani, "Do facts and Fiction Mix?, *New York Times Book Review*, Jan. 27, 1980.

2. Emile Zola, *Du Roman Experimental*, Chapter 1, Le Roman Experimental (1880) transl. Belle M. Sherman (New York, 1893); quoted in Miriam Allott, "The Novel as a Portrait of Life," *Novelists on the Novel*, (London: Routledge and Kegan Paul, 1965), 70.

3. "Raj Reversal," *Sunday*, 4-10 Dec. 1988, 30.

4. Richard F. Burton, transl. *The Arabian Night's Entertainment or The Book of a Thousand and One Nights* (New York: Random, 1932).

5. Nancy E. Batty, "The Art of Suspense: Rushdie's 1001 (Midnights)" *Ariel*, Vol. 18, Number 3, July 1987, The University of Calagary Press, 94.

6. *Ibid.*

7. "In Good Faith," *Sunday*, 25 Feb., 3 March 1990, 90—Rushdie's defence of *The Satanic Verses*.

8. Salman Rushdie, "Not Guilty!" *Sunday*, 18-24 Feb. 1990, 27.

9. Dr. Alistair Niven, "Indian Writing in English: Past and Present," Sahitya Akademi International Seminar, *Indian Literature in English and English Translation*, Feb. 25-28, 1986, India International Centre, New Delhi—"...he (Rushdie) has brought back into English fiction a sense of the panoramic...."

10. In an interview, Rushdie himself tells us that he is convinced of the existence of the supernatural world. 'Network East,' BBC-2, Sept. 24, 1988.

11. Rushdie, as he himself tells us, was actually born in June 1947—Interview with Rushdie, *The Sunday Observer*, Sept. 6, 1987. In the novel, Rushdie changes the date for narrative expediency. This is an instance of "fictionalizing" fact.

12. Salman Rushdie, *Midnight's Children* (London: Picador, 1982), 1-2.

13. Mentioned on the blurb of *The Satanic Verses* (London: Viking, 1988).

14. *Midnight's Children*, 462.

15. *Ibid.*, 9.

16. *Ibid.*, 166.

17. *Ibid.*, 356.

18. D.H. Lawrence, *Studies in Classic American Literature*, Chapter I—"Never trust the artist. Trust the tale. The proper function of the critic is to save the tale from the artist who created it."

19. *Midnight's Children*, 9.

20. C.S. Lewis, *An Experiment in Criticism* (London: Cambridge University Press, 1961), 50 "As a literary term a fantasy means any narrative that deals with impossibles and preternaturals."

21. *Ibid.*, 59; Lewis refers to the "realism of content" and the "realism of presentation." The two, according to him, are independent of each other. Rushdie's, one would feel, is more the "realism of presentation" than the "realism of content" though the contents, too, may be interpreted at a different level of psychological realism.

22. *Midnight's Children*, 167.

23. *Ibid.*, 75.

24. P. Syal, "'*Midnight's Children*,'" *New Quest*, Nov.-Dec. 1982, 349.

25. *Midnight's Children*, 47.

26. *Ibid.*, 200.

27. R.S. Pathak, "History and The Individual in the Novels of Rushdie," *Three Contemporary Novelists*, ed. R.K. Dhawan (New Delhi: Classical Publishing Company, 1985), 217.

28. *Midnight's Children*, 200.

29. Rita Joshi, "Fantasy as Reality: The Art of Salman Rushdie," *The Sunday Observer*, April 12, 1987.

30. *Midnight's Children*, 195.

31. *Ibid.*, 19.

32. *Ibid.*, 384.

33. *Ibid.*

34. *Ibid.*, 427.

35. *Ibid.*, 200.

36. *Ibid.*, 244.

37. C.D. Narasmhaiah in "Spurious Reputations: Vikram Seth, Rushdie and Tharoor," *Essays in Commonwealth Literature* (Delhi: Pencraft' International, 1995), 125, refers to Rushdie as "a juggler of words."

38. V.K. Suryanarayan Murti, "Secular Fantasy: Salman Rushdie's Fiction," *Kohinoor in the Crown: Critical Studies in Indian English Literature* (New Delhi: Sterling Publishers, 1987), 177.

39. Salman Rushdie "In Good Faith," *Sunday*, 25 Feb., 3 March 1990, 91.

40. *Ibid.*, 92.

41. Nancy E. Batty, *op. cit.*, *Ariel*, July 1987.

42. K. Raghavendra Rao, "The Novel as History as 'Chutney': Unriddling Salman Rushdie's 'Midnight's Children,'" *Perspectives of Indian Fiction in English,* ed. M.K. Naik (New Delhi: Abhinav Publications, 1985), 157.

43. *Midnight's Children*, 291.

44. *Ibid.*, 287.

45. *Ibid.*, 290.

46. "'Midnight's Children'—Memory's Recesses," *Northern India Patrika*, Sunday, Jan. 16, 1983, 1, 3.

47. "Raj Reversal" *Sunday, op. cit.,* 29.

48. Graham Hough, "The Novel and History," *An Essay on Criticism* (London: Duckworth, 1966), 114. "We should be wrong, however, to judge a novel by the amount of social and historical reality that it incorporates. It is not a quantitative matter."

49. P. Syal, *op. cit., New Quest,* 349.

50. David Lodge, "The Novelist at the Cross Roads," *The Novel Today,* ed. Malcolm Bradbury (Great Britain: Fontana, 1977), 85.

51. Damian Grant, *Realism,* The Critical Idiom Series (London: Methuen, 1970), 9. Compare Grant's theory of correspondence and coherence: "...the correspondence theory refers automatically to the fact, and requires that truth be verified by reference to it. In the coherence theory...truth is not earned by the labour of documentation and analysis, but coined, a ready synthesis."

52. William Styron's interpretations on history: quoted in Michiko Kakutani's "Do Facts and Fiction Mix? *The New York Times Book Review,* Jan. 27, 1980, 28.

53. Salman Rushdie, *Imaginary Homelands* (London: Granta Books, 1991), 10. Rushdie writes of his "urge to reclaim" his childhood years in *Midnight's Children.*

54. J.M. Waghmare, "Chinua Achebe's Vision of the Crumbling Past," *Indian Readings in Commonwealth Literature,* Amur *et al.,* 117.

55. Henry James, "The Art of Fiction," *The Theory of the American Novel,* ed. George Perkins (U.S.A.: Holt, Rhinehart and Winston, 1970), 178.

56. Quoted in *The Theory of the American Novel,* ed. George Perkins, xxxi; compare Graham Hough, *op. cit.,* 111 "...veridical imitation of objects in the real world is not the purpose of literature;...."

57. K. Raghavendra Rao, *op. cit.*

58. *Midnight's Children,* 459.
    The novel, however, is not to be taken as a sacrosanct version of the life of the novelist, for Rushdie himself guides our interpretation of the novel. In an interview (*Northern India Patrika,* Jan. 16, 1983), he voices his opinion regarding the

autobiographical element in the book—"It is entirely possible for a novel to be autobiographical and also to be completely fictional. That's what my book is. It comes very closely and directly out of the city and the places I remembered but there are only one or two characters in that book I would admit as portraits. Probably the most direct portrait is a street singer whom I remember from my childhood, but even he, in the book, becomes the parent of Saleem's alter-ego, Shiva, and certainly nothing of that nature happened in real life."

59. *Ibid.*, 461.

60. *Ibid.*, 459.
    Cf. George Watson, "Tense and Time," *The Story of the Novel*, (London: Macmillan, 1979), 73. Watson refers to a "Wordsworthian intuition that memory is imperfect."

61. *Ibid.*, 270.

62. *Ibid.*

63. *Ibid.*, 295.

64. Book Review of *Midnight's Children, The Sunday Standard*, 14 June 1981, 6.

65. Shyam M. Ansani, "The Socio-Political Scene of the 1930s: Its Impact on the Indo-English Novel" *Commonwealth Quarterly*, Vol. 6, No. 21, Dec. 1981, 15.

66. *Midnight's Children*, 420.

67. *Ibid.*, 122—Jawahar Lal Nehru, in his letter to Baby Saleem, wrote: "We shall be watching over your life with the closest attention; it will be, in a sense, the mirror of our own."

68. *Ibid.*, 118.

69. *Ibid.*, 9.

70. *Ibid.*

71. *Ibid.*

72. *Ibid.*, 86.

73. *Ibid.*, 122.

74. Shirley Toulson in *Contemporary Novelists*, ed. James Vinson (London: St. James press, 1972), 118, while referring to John Berger's novel, G., speaks of the novelist's objective of "depicting how each one of us is history in that we are both monumentally shaped by events, and in small measure, by the mere act of inhabiting our skins, influence their course."

75. *Midnight's Children*, 130.

76. *Ibid.*, 463.

77. *Ibid.*, 172.

78. *Ibid.*, 168.

79. *Ibid.*, 173.

80. *Ibid.*, 173.

81. *Ibid.*, 241.

82. *Ibid.*, 385.

83. *Ibid.*, 410.

84. *Ibid.*, 420.

85. *Ibid.*, 422.

86. *Ibid.*

87. *Ibid.*, 422.

88. *Ibid.*, 436.

89. *Ibid.*, 432.

90. *Ibid.*, 434.

91. *Ibid.*, 442.

92. *Ibid.*, 385.

93. Gordon Wise, Interview with Salman Rushdie, *Gentleman*, Feb. 1984, 59.

94. Interview, *Gentleman*, February 1984, 57.

95. *Midnight's Children*, 463.

96. Keith Wilson, "Midnight's Children and Reader Responsibility," *Critical Quarterly*, Vol. 26. No. 3, Autumn, 1984, 23.

97. B.K. Joshi, "It May be Long, but its Not Overwritten, *The Times of India*, 1 Nov. 1981, 8.

98. *Midnight's Children*, 435.

99. T.S. Eliot, *Selected Prose*, ed. John Hayward (Harmonds Worth: Penguin, 1963), 22-23: An individual with a consciousness of history is also "conscious of his place in time, of his own contemporaneity." However, an individual is an entity in his own right and should avoid "purpose" or aspirations regarding political life for as Rushdie in *Midnight's Children* observes, politics is a "bad dirty business" (435).

100. Levi Strauss: "...self-knowledge may only be achieved after establishing a critical distance on one's reality; cited by Flora

Gojnzales, "El Recurso Del Metodo," *The Centennial Review,* Vol. XXX, No. 2, Spring, 1986, 251.

101. Carl R. Mentley, "The Hermeneutic Project of Octavio Paz," *The Centennial Review,* Vol. XXX, No. 2, Spring, 1986, 156-57. "We all encounter our own self, our own being in the community of the other." Compare Marxism: The individual is seen in close relation to historical and socio-political events.

102. *Midnight's Children,* 165.

103. *Ibid.,* 435.

104. *Ibid.,* 149.

105. *Ibid.,* 226.

106. Walter Allen, *Reading a Novel* (Great Britain: Penguin, 1971), 18-19.

107. *Ibid.,* 18.

108. *Midnight's Children,* 238.

109. *Ibid.*

110. *Ibid.*

111. *Ibid.*

112. *Ibid.*

113. *Ibid.,* 238.

114. *Ibid.*

115. *Ibid.*

116. Henry James, "The Art of Fiction," *The Theory of the American Novel,* 185. "...I may therefore venture to say that the air of reality (solidity of specification) seems to me the supreme virtue of a novel—the merit on which all its other merits (including that conscious moral purpose of which Mr. Besant speaks) helplessly and submissively depend."

117. T.S. Eliot., *op. cit.,* 22.

118. *Midnight's Children,* 459.

119. *Ibid.,* 461.

120. *Ibid.,* 460.

121. *Ibid.*

122. *Ibid.*

123. *Ibid.*

124. *Ibid.*

125. *Ibid.*

126. *Ibid.*, 461.

127. *Ibid.*, 211; Rushdie, when interviewed by the B.B.C., referred to *Midnight's Children* as "a novel of memory"—Network East; B.C.2, 24 September 1988. Again in 'Midnight's Children: Memory's Recesses,' his interview published in the *Northern India Patrika*, January 16, 1983, 103, Rushdie speaks of the novel as being "about memory as well as being a novel of memory;" he further explains "It is about the way memory operates when you recall your life."

128. *Ibid.*, 211.

129. Cf. Carlos Fuentes, "Modern Literature Conference: The Politics of Experience," *The Centennial Review*, Vol. XXX, No. 2, Spring, 86, 135. "It is important to realize that we remember in the present, that memory is a celebration of the present. It is in the present that we remember and we desire which are two things that come together in writing—memory and yearning. Wanting, Trying to identify with something."

130. Nancy E. Batty, *op. cit.*, 61.

131. Salman Rushdie, "Not Guilty!" *Sunday*, Feb. 1990, 27.

132. Salman Rushdie, Interview, B.B.C., Sept. 2, 1988.

133. *Ibid.*

134. V.K. Suryanarayan Murti, *op. cit.*, 71.

135. *Ibid.*

136. Dr. Alistair Niven, *op. cit.*

137. *Ibid.*

138. Cited in Bryan Appleyard, "Portrait of the Novelist as a Hot Property." *The Sunday Times. Magazine*, Sept. 11, 1988, 31.

139. Cited *by* Bryan Appleyard, *op. cit.*, 28.

140. Ashutosh Banerjee, "Narrative Technique in 'Midnight's Children,'" *Three Contemporary Novelists*, ed. R.K. Dhawan, 196.

141. *Midnight's Children*, 9.

142. M.K. Naik, "A Life of Fragments: The Fate of Identity in Midnight's Children," *Studies in Indian English Literature*, (New Delhi: Sterling Publishers, 1987), 51.

143. *Ibid.*, 52.

144. M.K. Naik, *op. cit.*, 54.

145. Nancy E. Batty, *op. cit.*, 53.

146. *Midnight's Children*, 38.

147. Gerard Genette, *Narrative Discourse: An Essay in Method*, 1972, transl. Jane E. Lewin (New York: Cornell Press, 1980); there is an implication regarding the "constructedness" of all narrative.

148. Nancy E. Batty, *op. cit.*, 60.

149. *Ibid.*, 59.

150. *Midnight's Children*, 384.

151. Salman Rushdie "Midnight's Children: Memory's Recesses;" *Northern India Patrika*, January 16, 1983, 3.

152. *Ibid.*

153. *Midnight's Children*, 9.

154. *Ibid.*, 166.

155. *Ibid.*, 350.

156. *Ibid.*, 383.

157. *Ibid.*, 9.

158. *Ibid.*, 463.

159. *Ibid.*

160. The novel clearly appears to be a sublimation of Rushdie's sense of a loss of identity and we have in it 'the constant transformation of what would be "suffering" into works of art for the possibly higher experience of being "transparent"—that is an artist'—John Updike ed. David Thoburn and Howard Eiland, *Twentieth Century Views* (New Jersey: Prentice Hall, Inc., 1979).

161. Salman Rushdie, *op. cit.*, Interview, *Northern India Patrika*, January 16, 1983.

162. Cf. Flaubert—"I have always forbidden myself to put anything of myself into my work, and yet I have put in a great deal." cited by Robert Lidell, *A Treatise on The Novel*, (1947; rpt. London: Jonathan Cape, 1953), 104.

163. Salman Rushdie, *Imaginary Homelands*, 9.

164. Vassily Novikov, *Artistic Truth and Dialectics of Creative Work* (Moscow: Progress Publishers, 1981) Mark, the difference between "verisimilitude" and "truthfulness."

165. Robert Alter, "History and the New American Novel."

166. Salman Rushdie, "'Midnight's Children'—Memory's Recesses," *Northern Indian Patrika*, January 16, 1983, 6.

167. Tom Wolfe, "The New Fiction: Interview with Innovative American Writers" ed. David University of Illinois Press Publication, *The American Review*, Summer, 1976.

168. Vassily Novikov, *Artistic Truth and Dialectics of Creative Work*, 18. Cf. Lenin "Art does not require the recognition of its works as reality." Lenin, *Collected Works*, Vol. 38, 73.

169. Milan Kundera, *The Art of the Novel* (transl. Linder Asher Faber) quoted in *Times Literary Supplement*, June 24-30, 1988.

2

Salman Rushdie's *Midnight's Children*: A Reappropriation of India's Recent Past

FLORENCE D'SOUZA

The canonical, sacred texts of Hinduism are divided into two categories—a sum of learning believed to have been directly revealed to the hearing or *shruti* of the learned seers of India on the one hand, and on the other hand, recollections, commentaries, instructions for moral conduct, and reformulations of precepts already known, through memory or *smriti*. Both these bodies of ancient learning, the *shruti* texts of revelation and the *smriti* texts of recapitulation and commentary were transmitted orally for generations from teachers to their disciples in the sacred language of Sanskrit, before being compiled in a written form.[1] Since these texts were transmitted in Sanskrit, the language reserved for the exclusive use of the Brahmins, popular Indian traditions devised numerous ways of adapting them in the vernacular languages practised by the common people throughout India, in the form of legends, folktales, theatrical improvisations, sung verses, etc. Thus the ancient narratives, cosmogonies and moral precepts of the "high" cultural tradition of the Sanskritised, Brahminical kind have always had "low" cultural adaptations in the multitude of languages spoken and understood by the ordinary, non-Brahmin population.

This vital gesture of appropriating established symbols and collective representations in order to endow them with a local pertinence or a personalised meaning has been analysed by Roland Barthes in his *Mythologies*.[2] Barthes presents the two-tiered functioning of contemporary myths as a metalanguage that reinvests specific signs within an existing semiological system of signs with a new meaning—an emblematic, subversive, symbolic or composite meaning—in order to compensate for a feeling of alienation and instability in relation to knowledge and reality. Barthes underlines the possible subversive or poetic impact of this excessive, aesthetic gesture of remythologising accepted signs and respresentations. Although this does not naturally open on to revolutionary action, most often it does permit a subjective appropriation of history and reality, together with a sarcastic or humorous acceptation of an often alienating state of circumstances.

An example of Barthesian remythologisation of accepted signs can be observed in the verses of a vernacular Marathi poet of the 14th century named Nivrittinath, a disciple of Namdev, who was of the tailor caste. Namdev and Nivrittinath expressed their devotion for Lord Vitthal, an incarnation of Vishnu, in devotional verse that establishes a direct, personal relationship between the devotee and the divinity. They are thus exponents of what is known as the Bhakti tradition in India, that was a reaction against the excessive ritualisation and monopolisation of all religious practice by Brahminical norms, taboos and Sanskritic mediation. An example can be observed in the "Psalm of the Sadguru" by Nivrittinath:[3]

> The Prakrit and Sanskrit languages are of the same essence;
> They both need a guru to decipher their old message;
> The Shastras voice the same thoughts as the Vedas did;
> The Bhakti teaching is the fulfilment of the *shruti*;
> In the terrestrial grotto the obscurities of the night sky become clear;
> Men, deluded by illusions, become wise;
> Nivritti says: according to my guru, Gayani,
> The whole world is a form of the unique God.

Namdev and Nivrittinath are thus instances of the living tradition that is still very much a part of India today, thanks to constant reappropriations, readaptations and remythologisations.

In this paper I will try to trace Rushdie's application in *Midnight's Children*[4] of this subversive, Barthesian, remythologising gesture that is at least as old as the Bhakti tradition in its practice in India. I will proceed first by looking at the individual narrator's attempts to personally appropriate history and collective memory in order to create a place for himself in the general scheme of things. Then, I will follow his attempts to incorporate the social level (in particular his family and various religions) into his remythologised view. And finally, I will touch on Rushdie's narrator's attempts to endow historical events at the national level with a remythologised meaning. Very often, these remythologising investments of existing figures, symbols, institutions and events take on a syncretic turn that has the effect of avoiding univocity and making impossible the absolute locking of meaning in any single version, in an attempt to somehow make sense of things.

To begin with the individual narrator, Saleem Sinai's attempts in *Midnight's Children* to chart himself in on the map of the novel's bubbling narrative, they seem to cluster around two themes—his birth and his mission in life. Both appear with Messianic overtones giving him not only an individual, human role, but a metaphyscial, cosmic role as well. For example, Saleem Sinai's birth is preceded by an announcement of his arrival that could be read as an allusion to the Annunciation of the birth of Jesus by the Angel Gabriel, or the prophecy of the coming of Zoroaster, or the foretelling of the birth of the Buddha. However, here it is not some outside agent or angel who makes the announcement, but Saleem Sinai's own mother, Amina Sinai. Far from having any divine inspiration as its cause, Amina Sinai's announcement has the very concrete motivation of preventing the lynching of a Hindu peddler of a peepshow by an angry Muslim crowd (*MC* 76-77). Being a Muslim herself, she steps "between the mob and its prey" and while giving shelter to the peddler, Lifafa Das, challenges the crowd to attack her, "a mother who will have a child," in place of Lifafa Das. The narrator's comment on this episode underlines its ambivalence, since on the one hand it appears as a debunking of divine heraldings of the comings of Messiahs, and yet, on the other hand, sets the tone in advance for Saleem's participation in the history of his nation (*MC* 77): "From the moment of my conception, it seems, I have been public property." The prophecy of Ram Ram Seth, the fortune-teller, about the future of Amina Sinai's unborn child, takes an appropriately oracular form but can only make sense in the light of later events, remaining an obscure riddle in Chapter 6 of Part One (*MC* 87). Other prophecies are also associated with Saleem Sinai's birth. A few hours before this event, a sadhu or holy man named Purushottam, entered the garden of the Sinai family's Buckingham Villa in Bombay and installed himself beneath the garden tap in anticipation of "the coming of the One. The Mubarak—He who is Blessed" (*MC* 113). Another prophetic motif linked to Saleem's destiny is a painting left on Saleem's childhood bedroom wall by the former English owner Methwold—of Walter Raleigh as a boy "gazing rapturously" at an old fisherman seated on driftwood and pointing out to sea with his finger "while the young Raleigh listened to his tales" (*MC* 15, 79). The image of the fisherman's pointing finger recurs several times, always as an indication of "a thing concealed just over the horizon," and associating Saleem's path with that of the intrepid pioneer, Walter Raleigh (*MC* 79, also 74, 76, 127, 237, 442, 458). Much later in the text, Saleem undergoes a second birth of mythical dimensions, when, after the death of most of the members of his Aziz-Sinai family in Pakistan in 1965, he is reborn in India after the Bangladesh war of 1971. This is thanks to the magician's gifts of another midnight's child, Parvati-the-Witch. She spirits Saleem into Delhi from Bangladesh in her magician's wicker basket. This emergence from "the basket of invisibility" is accompanied by Saleem's rebellion against inevitability and a desire "to choose my own, undestined future" (*MC* 383). Again, an old woman, named Resham Bibi, who, in a parodic manner, echoes the three witches in Shakespeare's *Macbeth*, bewails Saleem's arrival in the magicians' ghetto in Delhi as an omen of "desolation, pestilence and death," since "this man is born twice, and not even from woman" (*MC* 387).[5]

This reference to his emergence from the magician's wicker-basket has resonances of Moses being found in the Nile in a wicker-basket by Pharaoh's daughter, the princess of Egypt.[6] It also has similarities with the baby Krishna being spirited away by Gargacharya from the prison where his parents, Vasudeva and Devaki of the Yadava community, were detained at the time of Krishna's birth. Gargacharya carried Krishna in a basket covered with flowers, in order to confide him to foster parents, Nandaraja and Yashoda, among the Gopas in Gokula.[7] However, the decrepit Resham Bibi's bodings of ill are disproved by a series of fortunate happenings and achievements in the magicians' ghetto after Saleem's arrival, leading to Saleem being dubbed "Saleem Kismeti, Lucky Saleem" (*MC* 387).

Another personal detail with remythologising reverberations is the childhood tin globe containing a newspaper photograph of the "midnight's child" Saleem on the historical day of his birth (15th August 1947) and a letter from India's first Prime Minister, Nehru, personally congratulating Saleem on "the happy accident" of the moment of his birth (*MC* 119, 122). These three articles form an emblematic childhood souvenir which emphasises that Saleem "had been mysteriously handcuffed to history" (*MC* 9). At the departure of the Sinai family from Bombay for Pakistan in 1958, Saleem ritually buried them in the garden of Buckingham Villa among the cacti, since "they are all that has survived of my past" (*MC* 305). The discrepancy between these humble childhood memorabilia and "holy relics" like the Hazratbal hair of the Prophet conserved in a mosque in Srinagar, or the body of Saint Francis Xavier conserved in the Cathedral of Bom Jesus in Goa, underlines the narrator's mock-seriousness (*MC* 305). They reappear in the text upon Saleem's return to the Methwold estate in Bombay in 1978. One of the first things Saleem does is to dig up his "long-buried world," exactly twenty years later (*MC* 458). The crushed tin globe of the world thus plays the role of Saleem's material mark in the garden of his childhood family home.

Saleem Sinai's extraordinary mission in life is expressed through a series of parallels between him and various mythical beings. Concerning his gift of moving without being observed in and out of the minds of other people, a gift that enables him to establish contact with the 1000 other children, and especially with the 581 survivors, of the Midnight Children's Conference (*MC* 196, 207), as well as in his mysterious return to India from Bangladesh "cloaked in invisibility" (*MC* 381), Saleem Sinai compares himself to Haroun-Al-Rashid, the "legendary Caliph" of Baghdad, known to have moved incognito through the bazars of his capital (*MC* 218). Then, in an allusion to his paradoxical capacity to be drained of his body fluids and grounded unawares and yet to take flight from constraining circumstances through his imagination and the "voices" inside his head, Saleem Sinai jokingly abandons as a possible chapter title "The Gander," meaning the bird of Hindu mythology known as the "hamsa" or "parahamsa" on which the god Brahma is reputed to ride: "symbol of the ability to live in two worlds, the physical and the spiritual, the world of land-and-water and the world of air, of flight" (*MC* 223, 229, 304). It remains one of the suggested avenues of this multipolar, proliferating text.

Saleem in the role of a Man-dog, suffering from post-trauma amnesia, goes to Bangladesh as part of the Pakistani Army's Intelligence Units, under the name of "the buddha" (*MC* 345-59). After staying for the typically mythical length of time of 420 days in the house of his maternal uncle, Mustapha Aziz, in Delhi, Saleem Sinai renounced (under pressure from his uncle) the comforts of family and home and returned to the magicians' slum, "like a beggar into the world." This stepping out in solitude and poverty from material security puts Saleem Sinai on a footing similar to that of "Gautama, the first and true Buddha" (*MC* 397).

In a polyphonic development around his family name, Sinai, Saleem explores its mythical associations in ancient Yemen or Hadhramaut, among the mystical Muslim sect of the Sufis, together with the sinuousness of the serpent and the hallowed mount of God's revelation to Moses, and through the geographical topos of the desert, with prophetic voices in the wilderness. He thus illustrates the multiplicity of meaning possible in a single semiological sign, leaving the door deliberately open to ever new layers of significance, as if to refuse any possible victimisation or boxing in by titles (*MC* 304-05).

Listening attentively to all these farflung and often farfetched links, as Saleem creates a place for himself in his tale, his one-woman audience in the text, Padma, makes a down-to-earth statement that can be read as a humorous deflation of Saleem's pretentious "historical sense" of his own worth (*MC* 120): "...after all, everbody gets born, it's not such a big thing."

This brings us to the social level of the family and various religions in Saleem Sinai's remythologising gestures to give established figures and signs of history and collective memory, a particular, personalised sense. Concerning the family, I have selected only two characters, each respectively linked to a motif, in order to illustrate the narrator's attempts to weave them into *the* sense-making tapestry of his text. They are Aadam Aziz and the perforated sheet, and Saleem Sinai and the theme of reverse fertility.

The doubled initials AA and SS are obviously contrived and it is also not by chance that Saleem looks upon his maternal grandfather (in an undoubtedly patriarchal society) as the fountainhead of his family line. His supposedly biological parents, Ahmed Sinai and Amina Sinai, née Mumtaz Aziz, both have the initials AS, forming an appropriate stepping stone between AA and SS. Aadam, like the father of mankind in the Biblical story of creation, "set history in motion" (*MC* 12), when as a medical doctor earlier trained in Heidelberg, he was called on to treat the illnesses of Naseem Ghani, the daughter of a landowner in Aadam's native valley in Kashmir. He has two characteristics in common with his grandson—a large nose and a hole in the centre of himself, "leaving him vulnerable to women and history" (*MC* 10, 192). The comical detail of the perforated sheet with a hole seven inches in diameter, through which Aadam Aziz was forced to examine his future wife (*MC* 10, 23), comes around several times in the text. It constitutes an improbable family heirloom and seems to underline the importance of fragments over the whole by its perforated nature (*MC* 107). It is also present at the end of the novel which deals with the metatextual problem of how to end. Among the numerous options reviewed, there is a dream with a hilarious transposition of the perforated sheet (*MC* 461):

> ...because last night the ghost of Reverend Mother appeared to me, staring down through the hole in a perforated cloud, waiting for my death so that she could weep a monsoon for forty days....

The male ancestor is replaced here by his overbearing wife in Saleem's imaginings, and the emblematic perforated sheet attains a cosmic dimension.

Saleem Sinai has a problem with genealogy, since his narrative throws into doubt the authenticity of the blood link between himself and the two individuals (Ahmed and Amina Sinai) who claimed to be his biological parents. Due to a case of cradle-switching and certain philanderings by his likely parents, the "child of midnight" has four possible fathers (Ahmed Sinai, Nadir Khan, Wee Willie Winkie and William Methwold) and three mothers in fact (Vanita, Amina Sinai and Mary Pereira), (*MC* 117, 127). In addition, his legal father, Ahmed Sinai, appears to have no lineage, being an orphan and only half Kashmiri himself (*MC* 66). He is also presented as a rather unheroic figure, with "a gift for taking wrong turnings" (*MC* 72), being surrounded by "the stink of failure" in all his business undertakings (*MC* 201), and addicted to alcohol (*MC* 131, 332). He falls into a kind of dotage after a stroke (*MC* 331, 337). The lack of an inspiring paternal figure could perhaps explain, at least in part, Saleem's need for surrogate fathers (*MC* 108). Thus Saleem savours the attention of his childless uncle and aunt, Hanif and Pia Aziz, when they adopted him for five weeks, after he lost the phalange of a finger (*MC* 237). Again, in Pakistan, when General Zulfikar's own son Zafar is not up to the situation, his cousin Saleem is delighted to assist his uncle in a dining table simulation with pepperpots of a planned *coup d'etat* before his uncle's dinner guest, the future President, General Ayub Khan (*MC* 290).

Saleem felt he had thus "created a new father" for himself. Furthering the theme of "reverse fertility" (*MC* 243), after forced sterilization in Benares during the Emergency, Saleem married Parvati-the-Witch, who was already expecting the midnight child Shiva's baby (*MC* 404-05). Thus it is that Parvati's son, to whom Saleem gave his maternal grandfather's first name, Aadam, and his own family surname, Sinai, in fact, had no blood connection with Saleem. Nevertheless, Aadam Sinai has the same initials, AS, as Ahmed and Amina Sinai, taking a legitimate place on the Aziz-Sinai family tree. Like a true, concerned parent, Saleem hopes that his 'son,' Aadam Sinai, will duly reverse the "endless sequence of nefarious sons-of-the-great," especially since all sons "(high and low)" were statistically known to most often behave badly (*MC* 333-34). Aadam Sinai's wet nurse, in the post-Emergency relocated magicians' settlement, a *dhoban* named Durga, who seduced the magicians' leader, Picture Singh, with her "serpentine charms" (*MC* 445), reminded Saleem of his grandmother nicknamed Reverend Mother, because of her expansive flattening of Picture Singh, who seemed to be shrinking daily, exactly like Aadam Aziz. This "nostalgic echo" of Saleem's grandparents in the very couple who looked after Aadam Sinai when his mother Parvati died during the Emergency violence, and while Saleem was a prisoner in the Widows' home in Benares, establishes a zig-zag family line that underlines the chance billetings of individuals in unforeseeable circusmtances, defying logic and straightforward family ties (*MC* 446). This is corroborated by Saleem's disenchanted assessment of family ties on the whole: "Family: an overrated idea" (*MC* 396).

At the level of religion, Saleem Sinai again establishes unconventional links between different religious beliefs and mythologies in order to incorporate their diversity into a personalised set of figures and symbols. A certain irreverent irony can be perceived in all his allusions to religion. To his own Muslim background, the references are few and always associated with other religions or with non-religious activities. Aadam Aziz's Muslim devotions are disrupted by atheistic questionings after his medical studies in Heidelberg, qualified as "a hole" within his inner being (*MC* 12). In the course of his narrative, the narrator apostrophes the reader to note that "despite my Muslim background," he was "well up in Hindu stories" (*MC* 149). The only aspect of Ramzan fasts Saleem mentions is that his family went to the movies as often as possible during "the month of fasting" (*MC* 180), giving the fasting period a celebratory more than a penitential aura. The voice of the prophet in the wilderness occurs several times, linked to the narrator's inner "voices," (*MC* 163) to the destabilizing effect produced by a prophetic version of events (*MC* 211) and to the possibility of the prophet having to "roam the desert" and run the risk of being "swallowed up by history" (*MC* 305). In this way, Saleem Sinai situates his own narrator's calling in the same register as the calling of the prophet Muhammad, also linking it to other figures like Moses, Joan of Arc, and less-known Arabian prophets like Maslama in the Yamama and Khalid ibn Sinan. In a typically profane disjunction, faced with the cynical disbelief of his family circle concerning his own "voices," Saleem finally decides that since according to Muslim belief the only prophet yet to come was "the last prophet" whose role would be "to announce the End", he himself "had not after all been chosen to preside over the end of the world" (*MC* 168). He thus voluntarily descends from the plane of archangels to the humbler level of lesser mortals. The Midnite-Confidential Club in Bombay, towards the end of the novel, with its "Stygian darkness" and "nightmare pit" atmosphere, evokes a "descent into Jahannum," the Islamic equivalent of Hell (*MC* 453). And the emblematic holy site in Srinagar where Aadam Aziz returns to depart from this life, is a hill dominating Srinagar's lake with a temple of Sankara Acharya, also called the Takht-e-Sulaiman or Seat of Solomon by Muslims (*MC* 10, 31, 278), being thus syncretised by divergent religious practices.

There are passing references to Parsi religious practices, in particular, to a human hand chewed by vultures from the Parsi Tower of Silence that parodically falls on Ahmed Sinai's face from the sky in Delhi like a slap from Destiny (*MC* 91), and to

Cyrus Dubash's doting widowed mother conjuring her own son into the role of the Parsi Messiah, Lord Khusro Khusrovand (*MC* 266-69), illustrating the danger of fanaticism that stalks all practitioners of all religions at all times. Thanks to Saleem's Goan Christian ayah, Mary Pereira and the Cathedral and John Connon's Boys' High School, a Christian mission school run by the Anglo-Scottish Education Society, which Saleem attended in Bombay, he was aware of Christian beliefs and religious festivals (*MC* 103, 105-06, 153, 163, 223, 253, 269).

A large part of the novel's religious mythological references are to the abundant diversity of Hindu mythology. A fundamental opposition in the novel lies between the two main members of the Midnight Children's Conference—between Saleem and Shiva, who were both born closest to the midnight hour. The roles they play place them in positions similar to those of the Hindu deities, Shiva the Destroyer and Vishnu the Preserver, with Saleem in the position of Vishnu. This opposition emerges most clearly in the voices debate between Shiva and Saleem over their respective perceptions of the possible purpose of the MCC (*MC* 221, 255). Shiva gives priority to the world of things and to violence, whereas Saleem accords more importance to the idealistic world of dreams, to Humanity and to Art. This is fully in keeping with the popular Hindu beliefs which associate Shiva with procreation, asceticism and violent destruction, whereas all the ten avatars of Vishnu are an inspiration for lyrical poetry, art forms and varied expressions of love and devotion. Certain Shivaite symbols appear in the text in a deviated, reinterpreted form that subversively transposes them out of their initial religious context. For example, the ascetical Brahmin bachelor, Dr. Narlikar, whose gynaecological profession had naturally to do with procreation, launched into a land reclamation scheme in Bombay's Back Bay with tetrapods along the seawall as the icon of the scheme (*MC* 176-78). Shiva's emblems being a trident and a stone column representing the Shivalingam of priapic virility, the tetrapods quickly became the object of Shivaite prayers and worship. Ironically, this provoked Narlikar's ire and caused his death. In an appropriately fitting manner, Narlikar's body was taken to the seat of Shivaite devotion in Benares, for cremation (*MC* 178). There are other allusions to Shivaite symbols. For example, in October 1971, during the Bangladesh war, just as the Ganga river was born *from* a cascade flowing *from* Shiva's hair, so Saleem Sinai and three colleagues from the West Pakistani army obtain release from a nightmarish sojourn in the Sundarbans forest, thanks to an unrecorded tidal wave that mysteriously flushed them out of the tropical jungle (*MC* 358, 368). Then again in Benares, Saleem Sinai was not only imprisoned during the Widow's Emergency, but was also subjected to forced sexual mutilation at the Palace of the Howling Widows there. The irony is striking—Saleem loses his virility at the holiest shrine of the God of Virility. A further irony is that the character Shiva, as a loyal supporter of the tyrannical Widow, had undergone a voluntary vasectomy (*MC* 440). Shiva has among his consorts the often terrifying goddess Kali and the more benign goddess Parvati. Kali appears briefly in the text in a vision of "a monumental Hindu temple" in the midst of the Sundarbans, as a "towering statue of a black dancing goddess [...] fecund and awful" (*MC* 366). Strangely, this vision is blended with a simultaneous vision of four beautiful houris in the camphor garden of the Islamic Paradise. This merging of visions from very different traditions can be read as a subversively syncretic proliferation. The character Parvati-the-Witch is syncretised through her double role with Saleem and with Shiva in the text, whereas in the Hindu tradition she is exclusively the consort of Shiva, thanks to whom she is able to create the elephant-headed god Ganesh. Indeed, although Parvati-the-Witch is responsible for transporting Saleem from Bangladesh to the magicians' ghetto in Delhi (*MC* 381), it is with Shiva that she conceives her child, only to marry Saleem, who then raises Shiva's elephant-eared child as his own, even naming him Aadam Sinai (*MC* 420). Again, this is a remythologisation of orthodox Hindu mythology for the purposes of the narrative.

Saleem Sinai's interlocutor, as he spins his tale, is named Padma, which means lotus, and is one of the names used for the goddess Laxmi, a consort of Vishnu. She is portrayed as a pouting, objecting auditor and irreverently nicknamed "dung lotus" and "dung goddess" (*MC* 32, 193), as lotuses do indeed thrive in areas of moisture and slime. The rich variety of legends that surrounds the goddess Padma-Laxmi is rapidly mentioned by Saleem, who savours his auditor's return after a rebellious disappearance. The goddess is associated with Kubera, the god of sacred treasure, with the sacred rivers, with the tree goddesses, with the guardians of life and with the lotus that grew out of Vishnu's navel, while she is also considered as the Mother of Time (*MC* 194). Such a wealth of mythological detail concerning Padma is consonant with the multiplication of direct and indirect references to mythologies throughout the text, and can be interpreted simultaneously as an exploration of the richness of meaning in individual signs and as a debunking of too much meaning.

Precisely because of this baroque proliferation of religious details and meanings in his text, the narrator pays a tribute to those who are "tainted with Bombayness" and who prefer "the impure" (*MC* 310), since they are secure from the stifling restrictions of fanaticism or totalitarian absoluteness (*MC* 438), as embodied by the Widow.

In the third part of this study, I will look at historical events at the national level. Here again, Rushdie's narrator links national happenings to personal or family or local episodes, giving them a particular, private meaning. These "historical coincidences" between world or national events and personal events, (*MC* 27), not only debunk their solemnity but also give the narrator a personal point of entry and concern in the general goings-on of his narrative, thereby justifying its existence. For example, on 11th November 1918, the day the First World War ended, we learn that Naseem Ghani developed a headache, permitting Aadam Aziz to finally see her face through the perforated sheet and so complete his fall (*MC* 27). In Agra, on 13th April 1919, the day of General Dyer's butchery at the Jallianwala Bagh, Aadam Aziz was present on the site, but a sudden sneeze made him drop to his knees and so spared him from Dyer's men's bullets (*MC* 36).

Saleem's birth, on August 15th, 1947, made him one of the 1001 (a mythical figure implying infinity) Midnight's children. When 420 (again a mythical figure implying "fraud, deception and trickery," *MC* 196), of them died, 581 remained as a parliament in Saleem Sinai's brain. It so happens that there are precisely 581 seats in India's Lower House of Parliament, the Lok Sabha (*MC* 196, 207). So, the Midnight Children's Conference takes on a symbolic importance. Again, the events of the year 1956, such as the Suez crisis, the launching of Five-Year-Plans in Nehru's India, and the language riots that led to a redrawing of the provincial borders within India, are accompanied in the novel by the death of the gynaecologist Narlikar, the death of the wandering minstrel Wee Willie Winkie, by Saleem's ninth Birthday and his discovery of the "voices" in his head (*MC* 150, 158, 167, 176, 179; 169 and 172).

Further, in 1962, the war between India and China is mirrored in Ahmed Sinai's cardiac problems, causing his departed family to return to his bedside in Bombay from Pakistan (*MC* 294). India's defeat in the Indo-Chinese war is marked by the draining of Saleem's nasal fluids, leaving him feeling like a grounded Parahamsa (*MC* 304). The Indo-Pak war of 1965 results in the death of most members of the Aziz-Sinai family in Karachi due to some particularly unfortunate bombs (*MC* 342).

The 1971 Bangladesh war is recounted in the fantastic mode, with Saleem Sinai as the buddha, a Man-Dog in a dog-sniffing intelligence unit of the Pakistan Army. A personal note is introduced when the traumatic amnesia he suffered after the bomb blasts that exterminated his family in Karachi was miraculously cured and his memory restored to him as he sat cross-legged under a tree in the Sundarbans, when "a blind, translucent serpent bit, and poured venom into, his heel" (*MC* 364). Paradoxically, after this snakebite in the heel, the amnesiac buddha is suddenly able to recount stories about his past, although he still cannot remember his own name (*MC* 365). Mythologies of various traditions are rife with episodes concerning vulnerable parts of the anatomies of heroes. At the end of the Mahabharata, Krishna dies from a poisoned arrow in his heel.[8] In the Nordic epic about Siegried and the treasure of the Nibelungen, a small area between Siegried's shoulder blades remains unprotected by the magic blood of the vanquished dragons.[9] In Homer's *Iliad,* during the Trojan war, Achilles, after having killed Hector, is himself killed by an arrow in his heel, shot by Hector's brother, Paris, son of Priam.[10] However, here, the vulnerable heel is inverted, since in Rushdie's text, the buddha's heel becomes the means of his recovery. In legends about Gautama the Buddha, the occasion when Muchalinda, the king of the cobras, protected him from rain and wind with his cobra's hood, as the Enlightened One meditated under a tree, is famous.[11] Thus, the historical event of the 1971 war is personalised through Saleem's participation in it, and remythologised by the introduction of an emblematic mythological motif into Saleem's trajectory during this war.

The Emergency in India from 1975 to 1977, when Indira Gandhi suspended civil liberties and practised autocratic dictatorship, is portrayed in Saleem's narrative as "a six-hundred-and-thirty-five-day-long midnight" (*MC* 443). On the local, private level, this translates as a violent confrontation between the two rival children of midnight, Shiva and Saleem, between "knees and a nose" (*MC* 428), when in April 1976, under the pretext of civic beautification and slum clearance, Saleem sees "the joints of my nemesis thundering towards me" (*MC* 430). This is followed by Saleem's imprisonment and forced sterilization in Benares, while Shiva disappears from the text (*MC* 443).

As the novel draws to a close around 15th August 1978, Saleem's hypersensitive nose inhales mixed smells—on the one hand, "the excitement of the coming Independence Day," and on the other "more tarnished perfumes: disillusion, venality, cynicism" (*MC* 457). His analysis is dispassionate: "...the nearly thirty-one-year-old myth of freedom is no longer what it was. New myths are needed; but that's none of my business" (*MC* 458).

To conclude, in an overall assessment of *Midnight's Children,* Kumkum Sangari in "The Politics of the Possible" salutes Rushdie's audacious experimentation with the parodic and allegorical modes, as a step "toward more incisive descriptions of interpenetrative cultural formation."[12] Indeed, as Saleem Sinai appropriates established signs, well-known events and beacons of collective memory in the construction of his own attempt to make sense of things, his subversive remythologising gesture (in the Barthesian sense), results in a syncretic patchwork of India's contemporary history in which no single orthodoxy and no single interpretation holds absolute sway.

NOTES AND REFERENCES

1. See Simona Sawhney's article "Remembering the Veda: accumulations of interest" in: *JOUVERT,* Vol. 3, Issues 1&2 (1999), online journal at website: <http://social.chass.ncsu.edu/jouvert>. At pp. 1-2, Simona Sawhney describes these two categories of ancient Indian texts as follows: "While the Samhitas (collections) of the four *Vedas* along with the *Brahmanas, the Aranyakas* and the *Upanishads* comprise the body of Vedic or *shruti* literature, the epics as well as the Dharma Sastras and the Puranas are included in the more amorphous *smriti* category."

2. Roland Barthes. *Mythologies,* Paris: Editions du Seuil, 1957, 193-247, "Le Mythe aujourd'hui."

3. Shree Nanamaharaj Sakharé. *Shree Dnyandev Gatha*. Pune: Varda Books, 1990. See chapter on Shree Nivrittinathmaharaj, p. 23, abhanga 146. (Translation from Marathi into English, mine).

4. Salman Rushdie. *Midnight's Children*. London: Vintage, 1995 (1981). All references to this novel will include page numbers from this edition, preceded by the initials *MC* between parentheses.

5. Cf. Shakespeare. *Macbeth*, IV-i, 79-81. 2nd Apparition: "Be bloody, bold and resolute: laugh to scorn/The power of man, for none of woman born/Shall harm Macbeth."

6. See *Exodus,* Chap 2, verses 1-10.

7. See Pratap R. Parekh. *Krishna: Myth or Reality?* Bombay: Jaico Publishing House, 1980, 30-32.

8. See John Dawson. *A Classical Dictionary of Hindu Mythology and Religion, Geography, History and Literature.* Delhi: Rupa & Co., 1993 (1982), Article on Krishna, see p. 164.

9. See article on Siegfried, in: *Dictionnaire des Œuvres.* Paris: Laffont, Collection Bouquins, 1952, in 7 volumes, Vol. VI, 134-35.

10. Commelin. *Mythologie grecque et romaine.* Paris: Gamier Frères, 1960, 368.

11. See Jacques Brosse. *Le Bouddha,* Paris: Pygmalion, 1997, 39.

12. Kumkum Sangari. "The Politics of the Possible," in: *Cultural Critique.* Minneapolis: University of Minnesota, 1987, No. 7, 157-86, especially 180.

3

Midnight's Children: Fantasy as Matrix

MADAN M. SARMA

One of the various dictionary definitions of 'fantasy' is that it is 'a creation of the unrestricted imagination whether expressed or conceived' (*The New Penguin English Dictionary, 2000*). A literary work of fantasy is often seen to be characterized by strange and unrealistic elements. The apparent 'unrealistic' elements in a fictional work dominated by fantasy may give the impression that fantasy is motivated by a desire to escape from reality. However, fantasy may be deliberately used by the author not to escape but to transcend reality, to subvert it to create a more encompassing vision of reality. So fantasy may be consciously used as a device, as a method, as Salman Rushdie and so many postmodernist novelists do so often.

Rushdie himself has said: "I think of fantasy as a method of producing intensified images of reality" (Hoffenden 246). In *Midnight's Children* Rushdie, in fact, presents intensified images of reality as he sees it in the Indian sub-continent in the decades preceding and following India's independence. The disparate materials pertaining to those times of political upheaval, popular upsurge, growing optimism, and chaotic developments that often bordered on the fantastic could not have been woven together by any other method but that of fantasy.

It is obvious that Rushdie borrows the technique of storytelling from Indian folk tales and the epics. But there is a deliberate subversion of the purposes of folk tales and epics. Contrary to the predominantly moral and didactic concern of the creators of folk tales and epics, Rushdie appears to be amoral. Both folk tales and epics make liberal use of the fantastic in an attempt to entertain and to present a more complete and complicated vision of reality that emerges out of the apparent unrealistic and unbelievable, and often chaotic happenings. The truth value of incidents and characters of a world that blends fantasy and reality is not the primary concern of either the storyteller or the listener/reader. What becomes relevant is the underlying 'truth' or 'reality,' the images of which emerge from what they read or listen to. In Rushdie's novel, however, what is real, or, what is unreal, is often uncertain not only to the reader but also to the narrator himself. Or, the real may have so many facets as to blur reality itself. In a vast country like India with an immense variety of life-experiences and with constant mingling of 'great' and 'little' traditions that have their own visions of reality, facts often get fictionalized, truth often seems incredible. "Reality is a question of perspective, the further you go from the past, the more concrete and plausible it seems—but as you approach the present, it inevitably seems more and more incredible" (Rushdie 165). Rushdie's concern is basically the present. So incredulity that he creates with the incorporation of elements of fantasy is inevitable.

In *Midnight's Children*, through the mixing and juxtaposition of the realistic and the fantastic, which are the features of magic realism, Rushdie makes an attempt to understand and interpret the multi-layered and complex reality of the socio-political life of the Indian subcontinent. At the same time there is an attempt to relate the reality of the individual life to that super-ordinate, all encompassing reality.

At the surface level, *Midnight's Children* is the story of Saleem Sinai and the other children of India's historic midnight of August 15, 1947. At a deeper level, it is the story of an emerging nation, of Saleem's own country, trying to come into its own. The narrator tries to convince us, the readers, that there is an integral relation between the private destiny of an individual, Saleem Sinai, and the public destiny. Quite often the distinctions between private and public world disappear in the narrator's perception: "From the moment of my conception, it seems, I have been public property" (77).

The parallelism between the two destinies is apparent in such descriptions:

> At the stroke of midnight hour, while the world sleeps, India awakens to life and freedom.... On the stroke of midnight, Sinai brother, your Begum Sahiba gave birth to a large, healthy child: a son! (116)
>
> I am literally disintegrating.... I shall eventually crumble into (approximately) six hundred and thirty million particles of anonymous, and necessarily oblivious dust. (37)

In the protagonist's perception, the destiny, hopes, aspirations and frustrations of six hundred and thirty million Indians are intertwined with his. In his imagination Saleem sees himself as the force that set in motion certain historical developments in India:

> To the tune of my little rhyme the first language riots got under way. (192)
>
> I became directly responsible for triggering off the violence which ended in the partition of the state boundary. (192)
>
> ...the war happened because I dreamed Kashmir into the fantasies of our rulers.... (339)

Such obliteration or blurring of the distinction between private and public worlds and private and collective fates is a feature of fantasy.

The narrator-protagonist of *Midnight's Children* admits that his story or a major part of it "ends in fantasy" (326) because in a situation where reality ceases to exist, or is subverted or made invisible, where the truth is manufactured, fantasy is the only means of uncovering what is hidden. Fantasy is a device of tracing and uncovering what is hidden, as Jackson points out, "The fantastic traces the unsaid and the unseen of culture that has been silenced, made invisible, covered over and made 'absent'" (4).

The language of fantasy is not representational. Like any other postmodern fiction, the language of *Midnight's Children* is not representational. It does not represent facts or what is real; instead it fabricates facts and the real. At times the language becomes metaphorical:

> Nobody could remember when Tai had been young. He had been plying this same boat, standing in the same hunched position, across the Dal and Nageena lakes... forever. (14)

But, as the narrator observes, "Reality can have metaphorical content; that does not make it less real" (200).

Fantasy is marked by certain other features too. For example, there is a breach of chronology in the storytelling, a breach of temporal and spatial unities. Rushdie's tale weaves past and present. It begins with the mention of Salim's birth in 1947, then it looks back to the early years of the twentieth century, then briefly recalls Saleem's childhood experience, and then goes back to 1919 and Jallianwala Bagh. In between, one notices self-reflexivity in the narrator's deliberate attempts to lay bare the process of constructing the story, constructing his own version of the reality.

Another element of fantasy found in Rushdie's novel is the overt violation of what is accepted as possible or probable, true or fact. For example, like the Puranic characters, Tai the eternal boatman is ageless: "Nobody could remember when Tai had been young. He had been plying this same boat, standing in the same hunched position, across the Dal and Nageena lakes...forever" (14). In his poetic language, Rushdie describes the agelessness of and something of the eternal in Tai: "His face was a sculpture of wind on water..." (14). At the same time incredulity is naturalized by exaggerating what could have been partially true or factual. The boatman Tai gave up washing. "He took to drifting slowly past the Aziz household, releasing the dreadful fumes of his body across the small garden and into the house. Flowers died; birds fled from the ledge outside old Father Aziz'z window" (27).

An inversion of the elements of this world is a marked feature of fantasy. Rushdie resorts to this method in his novel very often. The midnight's children had mysterious magical powers. A boy could step into mirrors and emerge from any reflecting surface, another could eat metal; a girl could inflict physical wounds with her words, another's finger was so green that she could grow prize aubergines in the Thar desert (198). Saleem himself had a highly developed sense of smell. "You see his nose?...Yea, man, he can follow any trail on earth...he could smell the damn mines!" (349). Reverend mother Nasim visited her daughter's dreams, often found another dream within a dream. Salim had the ability to "get inside grownups' thoughts." "I wake up at the stroke of midnight with Mary Pereira's dreams inside my head Night after Night" (171). "One night I awoke on the stroke of twelve to find my grandfather's dreams inside my head" (188).

There is a deliberate attempt to subvert the conventions of realistic representation throughout the novel. "It seems that the late summer of that year my grandfather, Doctor Aadam Aziz, contracted a highly dangerous form of optimism.... He was by no means alone, because, despite strenuous efforts by the authorities to stamp it out, this virulent disease had been breaking out all over India that year" (39). This is obviously a reference to a real historical event, the Quit India movement in 1942, when it appeared that freedom was at hand. "This optimism epidemic had been caused by one single human being, whose name, Mian Abdullah, was only used by newspapermen" (40).

An attempt to reconstruct reality to produce strange and unfamiliar effect is made in the novel. Mian Abdullah's hum "Could fall low enough to give you toothache, and when it rose to the highest, more feverish pitch, it had the ability of inducing erections in anyone within its vicinity" (46). When assassins came to kill hummingbird Abdullah "...his humming became higher and higher," "out of the range of our human ears, and was heard by the dogs of the town" (47-48).

...Indians had been subjected to the green air of the Rann even longer than they; so in that sorcerers' world a crazy war was fought in which each side thought it saw apparitions of devils fighting alongside its foes... (335).

Through all these the 'unreality' of the confusing, amorphous reality of our times is foregrounded. Fantasy serves as a time-tested device for doing so. In a tropical country like our India, fantasy seems to be, as the narrator himself states, not an optional literary method, but an inevitable natural psychic process, of grappling with the truth and reality that seem to be forever fuzzy:

> Heat, gnawing at the mind's divisions between fantasy and reality, made anything seem possible; the half-waking chaos of afternoon siestas fogged men's brains, and the air was filled with the stickiness of aroused desires. "What grows best in the heat: fantasy; unreason; lust." (167)

WORKS CITED

Brink, Andre. *The Novel: Language and Narrative from Carventes to Calvino*. London: Macmillan, 1998.

Goonetilleke, D.C.R.A. *Modern Novelists: Salman Rushdie*. London: Macmillan, 1998.

Hoffenden, John (ed.). *Novelists in Interview*. London: Methuen, 1985.

Jackson, Rosemary. *Fantasy: The Literature of Subversion*. London: Routledge, 1981.

Rushdie, Salman. *Midnight's Children*. Vintage: 1995.

4

Third World Literature as National Allegory: Salman Rushdie's *Midnight's Children*

Shyam S. Agarwalla

Fredric Jameson has argued in "Third World Literature in the Era of Multinational Capitalism" (1986) that "All Third World texts are necessarily...allegorical, and in a very specific way: they are to be read as...national allegories." In fact, he has claimed, "Third World texts, even those which are seemingly private and invested with a properly libidinal dynamic, necessarily project a political dimension in the form of a national allegory: the story of the private individual destiny is always an allegory of the embattled situation of the public third-world culture and society" (Jameson 65).

The trope of the Third World and implicitly of "Third World Literature" was conceived in France. Barbara Harlow reminds us that it was first used in August 1952, when Alfred Savvy, a French demographer, wrote in France Observateur: "We speak all too willingly of two worlds and their possible wars, their co-existence, etc., often forgetting that there exists a third, more important, world, one which, in terms of chronology, comes first...this Third World, ignored, scorned, exploited, as was the Third Estate, also wants to say something" (Harlowe 6-7). Bapsi Sidhwa, the Pakistani Parsi novelist, objects to the trope of this Third World and poses a counter-question:

> Why this preoccupation with the First and Third World? To classify or forget people because it costs an effort to understand them? To assume we know them sufficiently?

> It is time we see people as human beings, whether they are
> in Ethiopia, Salzburg or Pakistan. The human race is too
> complex to be conveniently pigeon-holed, and to do so is
> dangerous for our entire world. (Sidhwa 703-04)

Whether the conception of the Third World is a sheet bend to
fasten the First World with it or a gatekeeping to prevent the
Third World flooding First World in all respects is polemic but
it is true that this conception has come of age. In 1952, the
Third World Literature, in its mirror stage development, had
believed in the teleology of a distinct, vibrant, pulsating,
literature, which would identify itself with "the wretched of
the earth." Today, according to Peter Nazareth, "To belong to
the Third World is therefore to accept an identity, an identity
with the wretched of the earth spoken for by Frantz Fanon, to
determine to end all exploitation and oppression" (Nazareth
XXI).

George M. Gugelberger broadens the scope of the Third
World Literature:

> The Fanonian definition is free of racial and geographical
> connotations; at the same time it emphasizes a particular
> *telos*, namely facilitating the ending of exploitation and
> oppression. Identifying with "the wretched of the earth"
> can be done by people who do not live within the
> geographic Third World. This implies a Third World
> potential for the writer who is not directly associated with
> the Third World, which geographic location, on the other
> hand, does not necessarily guarantee. (Gugelberger 511)

Frantz Fanon's monumental book, *The Wretched of the Earth*,
is, according to most writers and critics, the alpha and omega
of all Third World Literature.

This strait-jacketing of the Third World Literature in
Fanonian garment is not acceptable to many theorists. Barbara
Harlow's *parergon* for the Third World Literature is a counter-
hegemony discourse, one which is "participatory" in "the
historical process of hegemony and resistance to domination,
rather than formal and analytic" (Harlow 9). It may be safely
said that a great part of African literature is *resistance literature*.

I foreground Mahatma Gandhi and Ngugi wa Thiong'o in this *parergon*. Both of them have tried to forestall the hegemony of the colonial elites and bourgeois-nationalist elites by advocating abrogation or rejection of English education in India and Kenya, in the context of decolonizing Third World's mindsets. Ngugi was for the abolition of the English departments in the decolonized African countries. Gandhiji objected with some fervour to "the harm done by this education (English) received through a foreign tongue.... It has created a gulf between the educated classes and the masses. We don't know them and they don't know us" (Gandhi 16). Leela Gandhi writes how this non-deferral and unambiguous voice of resistance did not find much favour in postcolonial literary-cultural discourse, monopolized by the elites.

Gandhi and his literary revolutionary counterpart Frantz Fanon, in Africa, are "united in their proposal of a radical style of total resistance to the totalising political and cultural offensive of the colonial civilizing mission" (Leela Gandhi 19). They desired to reject "Orientalist" projection of "Third World" people, who rendered the "Orient" a playground for Western "desires, repressions, investments, projections" [Said 1991 (1997)[8]]. Similarly, Elleke Boehmer describes British colonialism as a "textural takeover" of the non-western world (Boehmer 19). Gauri Vishwanathan, in her brilliantly-researched book *Masks of Conquest* (1989), uses her ratiocinative argumentation to foreground the controlling mechanisms of imperial textuality.

The *resistance literature* in British colonial India was mainly in Bankimchandra's novels, including *Anandmath*, which mothered *Bande Mataram*, the national song; Saratchand Chatterjee's *Pather Dabi*; Subramania Bharati's poetry; Raja Rao's *Kanthapura*, not counting hundreds of writers of regional character.

The third *parergon* of Third World Literature is made by Paulo Freire, a Latin American theoretician, in *Pedagogy of the Oppressed*. He uses the term "banking education" for western education and contrasts it with *conscienticiàao* or conscienticization (Freire 57). Gugelberger conceptualizes the former for domination and the latter for liberation. Some "Third World Literatures" thematize liberation, which can be seen in a survey of colonial literature in Asia, Africa and Latin America.

Lastly, Augusto Boal, in "Poetics of the Oppressed," writes that it "is essentially the poetics of liberation: the spectator frees himself thinks and acts for himself! Theatre is action. Perhaps the theatre is not revolutionary itself; but have no doubts, it is a rehearsal of revolution" (Boal 155).

Summing up all these attempts at situating these parerga theoretically, Gugelberger concludes that Third World Literature is more "realistic" than "mainstream" literature: .

> By "realistic" I mean more *ad hominem*, more radical in the root sense of the term (defined by Mary as grasping things by the root which is man himself). This implies talking about men and women not in the abstract but in the here and now. "Third World Literature" is bound to be always overtly political (all literature is covertly political but "Third World Literature" foregrounds its political message). It is always conscious not only of the present but of the past and the future. It tends to be allegorical and didactic.... It is a fighting literature which speaks out against the traditional triad of oppression: gender, race, class. (Gugelberger 515)

Fredric Jameson's concept of all "Third World Literature" as "national allegory" and his attempt at theorizing it as an overt expression of the thematizing of the political as opposed to Western texts which are "politically unconscious" are in tune with the conclusions drawn by Gugelberger.

Gugelberger writes about the Third World Literature as "realistic." But some Latin American writers have used the concept of magic realism, in place of realism. This concept of magic realism received its most influential endorsement in the Nobel Prize acceptance speech of Gabriel García Márquez. He recorded facts—"in the past eleven years twenty million Latin American children have died before their second birthday. Nearly one hundred and twenty thousand have disappeared as a consequence of repression.... A country created from all these Latin Americans in exile or enforced emigration would have a larger population than Norway."[1] "In such a disorderly reality," Márquez explained, the "poets and beggars, musicians and prophets, soldiers and scoundrels" of Colombia had been forced to respond to one of the saddest and most productive challenges in modern literature: "the want of conventional resource to make our life credible."[2] Then conventional wisdom gave birth to magic realism.

This incredible narration of Márquez finds echo in Salman Rushdie's own industrious apprenticeship in Spanish American Literature, Stephen Henighan writes:

> The visions of apocalypse are analogous (Rushdie's "whirlpool" in *Midnight's Children* corresponds to García Márquez "biblical hurricane" in *One Hundred Years of Solitude*, 336) and similarly pessimistic, though the traits of "Third World" blight (overpopulation in India, isolation and decay in Colombia) remain peculiar to each nation's experience.[3]

Salman Rushdie, in his 1984 essay "Outside the Whale," says:

> This is why (to end where I began) it really is necessary to make a revival fuss about Raj fiction and the Zombie-like of defunct Empire. The various films and TV shows and books (about the Raj)...propagate notions about History which must be quarrelled with, as loudly and as embarrassingly as possible. ("Outside the Whale" 138)

The mimetic method of writing was colonial's ploy to colonize colonialist's mind, culture and literature. Rushdie defends magic realism:

> The magical realism of the Latin Americans influences Indian-language writers in India today.... It is possible, I think, to begin to theorize common factors between writers from the societies—poor countries, or deprived minorities in powerful countries—and to say that much of what is new in world literature comes from this group....
>
> This transnational, cross-lingual pollination is not new. The works of Rabindranath Tagore, for example, have

long been widely available in Spanish-speaking America. (*Imaginary Homelands* 68-69)

Richard Cronin also suggests: "The Indian English novel cannot be written by a simple realist, but only by a writer willing to flirt with fantasy, a writer ready to dally with the Bombay talkies."[4] Fantasy is not regressive, not a flight from reality. It originally arises in Freud's thought during the correspondence with Fleiss, in which the notion is associated with "the question of how subjects tie themselves ethically to each other and enter a socially viable world." Fantasy "always contains a historical reference in so far as it involves, alongside the attempt to arrest the present, a journey through the past" (Rose). Ralph J. Crane's absolute a *posteriori* critique of Rushdie's use of magic realism in his fictional works is worth noting:

> Rushdie's form of magic realism is one which mixes the old 'realistic' plot of external action, not only in time, but in the exaggerated specific time which is history, with the modernist sense of a moral internal action, or the exaggeratedly unreal action of memory and dream.[5]

Salman Rushdie is also indebted to Gunter Grass's *The Tin Drum*. Rudolph Bader finds similarity of techniques between *Midnight's Children* and *The Tin Drum*: the structuring of historical memory through photos and newspaper clippings, the exoticism of dwarfs, magicians, gypsies and cripples; the mixing of "fairytale style...court evidence, school essay, public speech and other variations of the narrative mode" until the effect is one of "simultaneity of past, present and future."[6]

Salman Rushdie, unlike his peers, R.K. Narayan, Raja Rao, and Mulk Raj Anand, heavily relies on ancient Indian oral narrative tradition in writing his fictional works. He acknowledges it to David Brooks:

> One of the strange things about oral narrative—which I did look at very closely before writing *Midnight's Children*—is that you find there a form which is thousands of years old, and yet which has all the methods of the modernist novel, because when you have somebody who tells you a

story at that length, a story which is told from the morning to the night, it probably contains roughly as many words as a novel, and during the course of that story it is absolutely acceptable that the narrator will even so often enter his own story and chat about it—that he'll comment on the tale, digress because the tale reminds him of something, and then come back to the point.... It seems to me that when you look at the old narrative and use it, as I tried to do, as the basis of a novel, you become a modernist writer by becoming a traditional one.[7]

When India gained independence from the colonial power she inherited some colonial legacies. Helen Tiffin explicates them: "...the use of the English language; legal codes; educational practices; philosophical and interpretative frameworks— frequently persist in formerly colonized cultures long before independence has been achieved. In many cases they persist, in widely variant and/or culturally hybridized and syncretic forms, in the present. The 'post' in the 'post-colonial,' then, to borrow Terry Eagleton's terms in relation to Romanticism, is not 'confidently posterior' to an epoch, but rather a 'product' of it."[8]

My study of *Midnight's Children* foregrounds the birth of Saleem Sinai in Bombay in the midnight hour of 15 August 1947, the birth of independence, and of a new generation of Indians. Saleem, like Hatterr in G.V. Desani's *All About H. Hatterr* (1948), is linked to the Western-educated in all the British colonies. "Biologically I am fifty fifty," says Hatterr, a statement echoed in Saleem's view of himself as a "half and halfer," "neither this nor that." The trope of Anglepoise light, which Saleem uses to write his story, suggests the divided sensibility in Saleem, a child born in postcolonial India, not post-Independence India. Hatterr writes of his "father European Christian-by-faith merchant merman (seaman), mother an Oriental...steady non-voyaging, non-Christian human (no mermaid)." Saleem is also half-English, the illegitimate son of a departing colonial agent. Hatterr, Saleem, born of the Indo-British culture, actually do not belong to a specific British tradition or Western civilization, but are products of colonial and postcolonial values, like Lady Chatterjee in Paul Scott's *The Jewel in the Crown*. All three lack true Indian sensibility which, in turn, is linked to the widely assumed loss of their 'identity.' Vasant A. Shahane explicates it: "The desire for identity is bound to be a middle-class burden since the very poor (and often the very rich) are not affected by it because it is primarily the heart of the middle-class person that burns over these issues and predicaments."[9] The predicament, of Hatterr, Saleem, Lady Chatterjee, even the Chatterjees of Vikram Seth's *A Suitable Boy*, is that they have lost the immemorial past of India and, therefore, of her civilization and its functionalism.

The unfree India gains the territorial legitimacy as an independent nation, in the midnight of 15 August 1947, with a stirring, literary and emotional speech of Pandit Jawaharlal Nehru:

> Long years ago we made a tryst with destiny; and now the time comes when we shall redeem our pledge—not wholly or in full measure, but very substantially.... (*MC* 134)

It is two minutes to twelve. Nehru goes on with his oratory: ...At the stroke of the midnight hour, while the world sleeps, India awakens to life and freedom.... A moment comes, which comes but rarely in history, when we step out from the old to the new; when an age ends; and when the soul of a nation long suppressed finds utterance..." (*MC* 134). At this hour, precisely on the stroke of midnight, Dr. Narlikar's Nursing Home "awakens to life and freedom;" a child steps out of the old womb; the soul of the child "long suppressed finds utterance" and a brand-new Indian, a rich compost of the colonized and the colonizer, adds his address to a long list of post-colonial Indians.

Like Nehru's *An Autobiography* written in the colonial period, Saleem would also write his own autobiography which would cover the period, 1919-1975, in half colonial and half post-colonial India. The birth of Saleem is a *kernel* event; the birth of Shiva is a *satellite* event and the birth of one thousand children, between 12 PM and 1 AM, is a *nuclei* event, in this novel. Dieter Riemenschneider observes: "There is virtually one event which is not given an individual as well as an historical meaning."[10] This observation of Riemenschneider conflates with Jameson. Is the birth of Saleem on the midnight of 15 August 1947, a coincidence or does it lead to an allegorical study of the colonial and post-colonial India? Is Saleem a national hero, like Gandhi and Nehru, who dominates every major event in post-colonial India? Is his autobiography as determinative as that of Nehru, in defining, directing, and qualifying the course of post-colonial India and its political structure?

First of all, I find the concept of nation in *Midnight's Children* problematic, as propounded in the postmodernist literary theory. Salman Rushdie himself explicates it:

A nation which had never previously existed was about to win its freedom, catapulting us into a world which, although it had five thousand years of history, although it had invented the game of chess and traded with Middle Kingdom Egypt, was nevertheless quite imaginary; a mythical land, a country which would never exist except by the efforts of a phenomenal collective will—except in a dream we all agreed to dream. (*MC* 129-30)

Rushdie, through the use of words like "imaginary" and "mythical" and the evocation of "the efforts of a phenomenal collective will" that dreamed India into being, emphasizes the imagined and willed aspects of nation-formation. In an identical anti-essentialist theory Benedict Anderson says: "In an anthropological spirit, then, I propose the following definition of the nation: It is an imagined political community.... Communities are to be distinguished, not by their falsity/ genuineness, but by the style in which they are imagined" (Anderson 15).

It is necessary that Mahatma Gandhi's absolute faith in an unified India be contextualized with Rushdie's. David W. Price's claim that "Mahatma Gandhi hardly appears at all" and that "primary emphasis on the great figures"[11] is avoided, is *petitio principii*. The role played by Gandhi in unifying

India during the Freedom Movement, according to Ernest Renan, was in presupposing a past of India: "It is summarized, however, in the present by a tangible fact, namely consent, the clearly expressed desire to continue a common life" (Renan 19). Rushdie says: "Gandhi dies at a wrong time" and there is a sense of loss and regret. Aadam's comment on *hartal* and Gandhi: "But this is India in the heyday of the Mahatma, when even language obeys the instructions of Gandhi" (*MC* 33) is to be contextualized with the *mantra* of *repression* that Gandhi chanted and which helped him to overdetermine the willed unity of India.

Salman Rushdie, on the contrary, problematizes India as nation, perhaps following the mind-reading of V.S. Naipaul or postmodernist literary theorists. Partha Chatterjee argues that "the processes of the modern state have taken root in the contemporary history of India. It is not the origins but the process of domestication of the modern state in India that is at issue; one does not, unfortunately, have the option of sending this state back to its origins."[12] I have written earlier that the Freedom Movement under the stewardship of Gandhi paved the way for the establishment of the modern state in India. What I said about the postcolonial India finds legitimacy in Partha Chatterjee's observation:

> What is curious is the way in which, despite the establishment of a postcolonial regime, an underlying current of thinking about the sociological bases of Indian politics continues to run along channels excavated by colonial discourse...the categories of the liberal-democratic state produced theoretically in the West, and...the categories that made up the Orientalist construction of India—are continually being re-created in ever more unrecognizable form.[13]

What Rushdie does is to revive the Orientalist construction of India, to cut out "majority and minority communities defined in terms of criteria such as religion, language, or tribe and applied over a variety of territorial units ranging from a part of a district to the country itself,"[14] from the larger body of a nation. He dresses out these cut and dried construction of

India with allegory and there are thus many Jamesonian "national" allegories in *Midnight's Children*.

Unlike Nehru in *The Discovery of India*, eliding all divisive forces into a lyrical unity, or Vikram Seth in *A Suitable Boy* imparting a sociological stability to India marked by deep political, economic and cultural divisions, Rushdie highlights divisive forces, shows Saleem negotiating a fragmented terrain of his inner and outer worlds. Rushdie himself specifies his idea: "(In *Midnight's Children*) the defining image of India is the crowd and a crowd is by its very nature superabundant, heterogeneous, many things at once" (Rushdie, 1998, 25). Here, one should seek out "national" allegories. Rushdie does not think that his novels are influenced by classical Indian allegory:

> I usually resist the idea of allegory. In India there's too much of it, allegory is a kind of disease. People try to decode everything, every story or text allegorically, and although clearly there are elements that you could call allegorical in *Midnight's Children* and *Shame*, the books are not allegories in the way that the *Pilgrim's Progress* is, where everything stands for something and the real story is a story that is not told. Allegory stands for something and the real story is a story that is not told. Allegory asks readers to make a translation, to uncover a secret text that has not actually been written. In that sense I don't think my books operate as allegories. (Rushdie, 1985, 107-08)

Saleem Sinai's birth in 1947 and his autobiographical odyssey in India till 1975 throw about some elements, which assume the shape of allegories. He is unable to assemble all these allegorical elements to encapsulate the whole of India. Nor are we. But I can, at least, assemble some pearls and weave them into a string of national allegory. For example, the description of Bombay is one such allegorical pearl:

> The fishermen were here first. Before Mountbatten's ticktock...and back and back, beyond Dalhousie and Elphinstone, before the East India Company built its fort...at the dawn of time, when Bombay was a

dumbbellshaped island tapering, at the centre, to a narrow shining strand beyond which could be seen the finest and largest natural harbour in Asia...in this primeval world before clock-towers, the fishermen...sailed in Arab dhows.... There were also coconuts and rice. And, above it all, the benign presiding influence of the goddess Mumbadevi... may well have become the city's. But then, the Portuguese named the place Bom Bahia for its harbour, and not for the goddess of the pomfret folk...the Portuguese were the first invaders, using the harbour to shelter their merchant ships.... (MC 105-06)

This passage reveals Saleem's alignments with the specificity of colonial and contemporary representations of Bombay. The genealogy of Bombay is in jumbled fragments. Jyotsna G. Singh's comment is indicative of its allegorical nature:

This narrative of the city typifies Saleem Sinai's rhetorical strategy as a historian and story-teller: not only does he embrace the multiple myths of Bombay's origins here, but throughout the novel his origins here, but throughout the novel his fragmentary mode of storytelling activates *multiple* conceptions of India and Indianness. Thus, the "reality" of the independent nation is imbricated in textual fragments of non-chronological, linear time, in which the colonial (and pre-colonial), past elides with the postcolonial present. And as readers, we share Saleem's inability to locate any essence or 'truth' about the nation.... (Singh 169)

Throughout *Midnight's Children* readers are in the throes of thought-reading of Rushdie about *multiple* conceptions of India and Indianness. The narrator's description of Bombay allegorizes them.

The narrator also writes about "Mountbatten's ticktock," the real time of the colonizer, repeatedly. Padma "heard Mountbatten's ticktock...English-made, it beats with relentless accuracy" (123). Methwold parodies Indian expression "Subkuch ticktock hai." The "ticktock" of Mountbatten and its parody by Methwold is an amnesia, not only of Saleem and India (post-colonial) but an amnesia that our colonial masters sought to impose upon us. Saleem explicates it by giving its Indian counter-version:

> (T)ime, in my experience, has been...variable and inconstant...no people whose world for "yesterday" is the same as their word for "tomorrow" can be said to have a firm grip on time. (*MC* 106)

The "ticktock" of Mountbatten or its "relentless accuracy" is the *connotation* of the imposition of colonial-minded discipline over India and Indians. This iron-bound discipline of "ticktock" runs counter to millennia-old Indian concept of time, which Richard Lannoy describes suggestively:

> (T)he Indian syllogism is the reverse of the Western: the notion of effect is formed first, and that of the cause is retrospectively inferred and started afterwards.... The thought-process itself is retrospective, cyclical.... For example, *parson* can mean either 'day after tomorrow' or 'day before yesterday,' while *atarson* can equally mean 'three days ago' or 'three days from now'.... A sequence of connected events, while it may be perceived lineally, is not valued in the same way as a *non-lineal pattern* outside history.[15]

Rushdie allegorises the linear time of the colonialists, as opposed to the circular time of timeless India. There is always a slippage between timeless India and postcolonial India, apart from a short subversive history of India. In the novel, Rushdie leads us to believe that Saleem is interpellating both.

Methwold's palace is another allegorical pearl in *Midnight's Children*. There are "four identical houses built in a style befitting their original residents.... William Methwold, had named (them) majestically after the palaces of Europe" (*MC* 108). The "allegory of this passage suggests the passing on of the political mantle to the Indian *petit bourgeoisie* which not only inherited political power from the colonial masters but also many of its peculiar colonial accoutrements after independence."[16] Buckingham Palace alias Buckingham Villa is our *Rashtrapati Bhavan*. Versailles Villa is our Parliament. Escorial Villa is allegorized for our educational modes and exclusive clubs. The postcolonial India, under the leadership of Pt. Nehru, retained all these relics of colonialism, disregarding Gandhi.

In continuation of the allegorization of the Methwold's palace, there is another twist to it. Methwold explains to Ahmad: "My notion is to stage my own transfer of assets.... Select suitable persons...hand everything over absolutely intact: in tiptop working order" (111). Goonetilleke puts "select suitable persons" in place, that is, Ahmad Sinai, Homi Catrack, Ibrahim Ibrahim, Dubash, Dr. Narlikar and Commander Sabarmati would act as carrier pigeons of William Methwold, who "would form the centre of my (Saleem's) world moved into the estate and tolerated the curious whims of the Englishman—because the price, after all, was right" (112). All of them are allegories for "the Imperial tradition of the British Raj" (David Price 96). Goonetilleke, on the other hand, allegorizes them in a different way from Price:

> ...but it seems to me that he (Methwold) is only attempting to control India through imposing Western patterns of culture—and, consequently, behaviour—on the power elite of post-independence India. Actually subtext has it that power has been transferred to those already inclined towards the West, the anglicized Indians.... Imperialism does not end when the imperialists leave. (Goonetilleke 26)

Edward Said, Ranjit Guha, Dr. Kwame Nkrumah, and Frantz Fanon agree to the rigidification of postcolonial middle class society, partly out of parasitical mindsets and partly due to colonial wiles and tricks.

I take up another example from the novel to essentialize what I said above. It is about the physical traits of Saleem and Shiva. Goonetilleke suggests:

> Saleem becomes a representative Anglicized, middle-class intellectual.... Shiva...represents the indigenous (predominantly Hindu) proletariat. His most prominent physical trait is his knees, suggesting strength, basis, foundation, someone nearer the soil. Saleem is not India, but a segment of India. So is Shiva. Nose is no whole, any

more than knees.... What the transfer of power means in terms of class (an important issue in postmodernism), is clear at the very birth of the nation. (Goonetilleke 28)

In another instance of national allegory, Rushdie's *narrative mood* aims at showing the mutual antagonism between Saleem and Shiva, which spells misfortunes for India.

The questions I'd (Saleem) been dreading and trying not to prove began: why is Shiva not here? And: why have you closed off part of your mind? ...when...the children of midnight launched a concerted assault on me, I had no defence...accusing me of secrecy prevarication, high-handedness, egotism; they tore me apart, because, despite all their sound-and-fury, I could not unblock what I had sealed away; I could not bring myself to tell them Mary's secret (that Shiva was the heir, the leader, and Saleem the bastard child of Methwold and Vanita)...now, as the midnight children lost faith in me, they also lost their belief in the thing I had made for them. I continued...to attempt to convene—our nightly session, but they fled from me, not one by one, but in tens and twenties; each night, less of them were willing to tune in... (*MC* 298).

Shiva has "the gifts of war (or Rama, who could draw the unarrowable; of Arjuna and Krishna; the ancient prowess of Kurus and Pandavas united" (200). On the other hand, Saleem meekly accepts the Prime Minister's letter to the Midnight Children. He narrates the magical properties of the nation's first children. He insists on maintaining the MCC as a loose federation of equals. His is the Euro-centric view of the Anglicized Indians.

The anti-essentialism of Shiva is absolute. He yells at Saleem: "For what reason you're rich and I'm poor? Where's the reason in starving, man? God knows how many millions of damn fools living in this country, man, and you think there's a purpose (263-64)!" The national allegory lies between two views, the endrocentric view of Shiva and the Euro-centric view of Saleem. The former privileges the subalterns. For them all big talks about election, five year plans, democracy carry no conviction. Shiva is one face of the subalternity, Padma is that of another. What I believe is that colonialism was doubtless a key, even decisive moment in the novel but "the history of sedimentations which *constitutes* the Indian cultural formation includes much besides colonialism *per se*" (Ahmad 172). Rushdie's Orwellian loveliness in politics prevents the elites and the subalterns to integrate.

Indira Gandhi's Emergency period is also allegorized in the novel. India's prominent newspaper *The Times of India* toed her rule. On the pretext of beautifying Delhi primitive method of bulldozing of slum houses were executed. The Sanjay brigade sterilized "magicians and old beggars" (512). The "Widow" was afraid of five hundred and seventy-eight midnight children. For them "a modern nation-state could have neither time nor compassion—twenty-nine years old now…were brought to the Widow's Hostel…their whispers began to fill the walls" (517). Saleem, who betrayed them, cannot count an exact number of Indians who lost their freedom: "either thirty thousand or a quarter of a million persons" (517). The Widow said: "It is only a small percentage of the population of India" (517). Saleem, in his autobiographical and sarcastic vein, says:

> All sorts of things happen during an Emergency: trains run on time, black-money hoarders are frightened into paying taxes, even the weather is brought to heel, and bumper harvests are reaped; there is, I repeat, a white part as well as a black. (*MC* 517)

Indira is glorified as a goddess. "…our Lady is a manifestation of 'the OM'" (521). Indira is India. Her supporters and some newspapers allegorize as *Bharat Mata*. She "aspired to be Devi, the Mother-goddess in her most terrible aspect, possessor of the *Shakti* of the gods" (522). This allegorical figure of Indira Gandhi is contingent and essentialist. This omnipotent Goddess is afraid of the magical children of midnight. She reminds me of Lord Indra, the chief of Hindu gods and goddesses, who, though omnipotent, used to tremble like a leaf in a tree, whenever a demon or a seer or an ascetic performed *tapasya* for gaining boons from Brahma or Shiva. He, in most cases, suffered from an imaginary fear of his displacement from Heaven and boon-gainers' placement there. Indira Gandhi's enthronement in the democratic polity of India as goddess or Lord Indra is symbolic of subcontinental leaders, the Pakistani Generals, the Communist Parties, the Naxalites, and the so-called prophets, who are out to impose political and moral amnesia on an entire nation. Rushdie always portrays himself as one of the lone individuals occupying a moral high ground *above* the 'chimeras of politics' (Rushdie's phrase).... In an earlier time, right into the heart of modernism, such desolations of the self were still experienced quite frequently as a loss: what postmodernism has done is to validate precisely the pleasures of such unbelonging, which is rehearsed now as a *utopia*, so that belonging *nowhere* is nevertheless construed as the perennial pleasure of belonging everywhere" (Ahmad 157). The existential self-questioning of Saleem is, therefore, that of Rushdie's "existential question: How are we to live in the world" (*IH* 18)? Saleem's "enabling and liberating (powers)... are now lost to the country's multitudes" (Syed 103).

Despite the elitist formation of postcolonial leadership, despite the ascendancy of Saleem over Shiva, the formation and activation of Sanjay brigade altered the moral map of Indian politics for ever. The *kernel event* of the birth and growth of Saleem becomes a *satellite event*; the *satellite event* of the birth of Shiva becomes a *kernel event*. The Indo-Pak wars in 1965 and 1971, the imposition of the infamous Emergency in 1975 finally demolish the elitist nature of Indian politics, and with it, Saleem. On the other hand, the subalternity of Shiva does not make him a meek inheritor of the age-old Indian culture and civilization. He becomes *arriviste*, the chief character in the Sanjay brigade. The Indian political scenario, since the arrival of Sanjay brigade, has become a stage where the Shivas rule the roost. They stride the nation space, strike strife and discord, rouse casteist and communal feelings, flout all norms of rule and decency, fluctuate in political alignments, and arrogate to themselves the power to dispense with human lives and state funds. Salman Rushdie, in *Midnight's Children* and *The Moor's Last Sigh*, allegorizes the triumph of *Adharma* over *Dharma*.

The "collective will" of Muslims, glued by religion, helped to create an "imaginary" land, Pakistan, in 1947. The "collective will" was collapsing in East Pakistan under the leadership of Sheikh Mujib. It felt oppressed and confined under the rigidification of West Pakistan. The former demanded secession from the latter. Language intervened between religious glueyness and Fascist rulers. The buddha (Saleem) catalogues a history of arson, loot and rape by the Fascist West Pakistan rulers on East Pakistan, which suitably culminates in the Indian army's arrival and Freedom, of East Pakistan. The map of South Asia is redrawn on the basis of language.

Similarly, the map of India is redrawn in 1956 on the linguistic basis. The state of Bombay witnesses the Marathi language marchers clashing with the Gujarati counterparts, in 1957. Saleem crashes into the Marathi marchers in 1957. He witnesses the partition of Bombay into Maharashtra and Gujarat; he also witnesses the partition of Pakistan into Pakistan and Bangladesh. As an allegory of Indian colonial and post-colonial history, *Midnight's Children* and *The Moor's Last Sigh* foreground marginal cultures and histories, interrogate nationalism and continue to produce divisions in India on the basis of language, caste, and religion. The narrator in *The Moor's Last Sigh* playfully poses a serious question at the time of impending partition of India: "Christians, Portuguese, and Jews; Chinese tiles promoting godless views; pushy ladies, skirts-not-saris, Spanish shenanigans, Moorish crowns...can this really be India? *Bharat Mata* (Mother India), *Hindustan Hamara*, is this place?" (*MLS* 87). Earlier, I had quoted Partha Chatterjee and I conclude that the satiric allegory of merging nationalism, unlike that of Nehru and Seth, is often protean and deadly entity. The myth of *Bharat Mata* is naïve and spurious. Rushdie writes:

> I remember when *Midnight's Children* was first published in 1981...it was too pessimistic about the future... suggestions of a new, pragmatic generation...now seem absurdly, romantically optimistic. (*IH* 33)

Aijaz Ahmad challenges Jameson's arbitrary imposition of national allegory on all 'Third-World texts' in "Jameson's

Rhetoric of Otherness and 'The National Allegory'" in his book *In Theory*. I cannot better it. Before I conclude, I would like to quote two important writer and critic. Wilson Harris says:

> Remember that allegory is one of the ruling concepts which our civilization has imposed on many colonial peoples, victimized peoples, let us say. But my assertion is that one can come to an allegory from that side, from the victimized side and renovate it, rediscover implications in it which make it genuine and true, so that allegory is not a museum piece.[17]

Mary Layoun says:

> ...in a perverse if nonetheless pleasing reversal, the most radical location or citation of the allegory of nationalism could perhaps not exclusively be situated in the Third-World novel at all but precisely in the universalizing postmodernist first-world text-works like Thomas Pychon's *Gravity's Rainbow*, E.L. Doctorow's *Ragtime*, Ralph Ellison's *Invisible Man* and many others.[18]

Vijay Mishra compares the allegory of *The Ramayana* with *The Mahabharata* and says:

> ...one finds that *The Ramayana*, read allegorically, affirms Hindu genealogy, order, and sanctity of the family and constructs the Indian ideals of man and woman; in contrast *The Mahabharata* is about power and politics, about national disintegration and schisms: the Indian here confronts the forces of history. Thus, not surprisingly, Indians see the former epic as "life-atoning" whereas they never recite *The Mahabharata* in full for fear that it would lead to disharmony and chaos. (Mishra 196)

Continuing this analogy, I can say that *The Discovery of India* and *A Suitable Boy* are *The Ramayana* and *Midnight's Children* is *The Mahabharata*, of postcolonial India.

NOTES AND REFERENCES

1. Gabriel García Márquez. "The Solitude of Latin America: Nobel Address, 1982," 208-09.

2. Márquez.

3. Stephen Henighan. "Coming to Benegali: The Genesis of Salman Rushdie's Rewriting of Juan Rulfo in *The Moor's Last Sigh*," in *The Journal of Commonwealth Literature*, Vol. 33, No. 2, 1998, 56.

4. Richard Cronin. "The Indian English Novel: *Kim* and *Midnight's Children*," *Modern Fiction Studies*, Vol. 33, No. 2, 1987, 205.

5. Ralph J. Crane. *Inventing India: A History of India in English-Language Fiction*. London: Macmillan, 1992, 187.

6. Rudolph Bader. "Indian Tin Drum," *International Fiction Review*, Vol. II (Summer, 1984), 76.

7. "Salman Rushdie: An Interview Conducted by David Brooks, 6/3/4," in *Helix*, No. 19/20, 1984, quoted from *Span*, No. 21, 1985, 184.

8. Helen Tiffin. "Plato's Cave: Educational and Critical Practices," in *New National and Post-colonial Literature*, ed. Bruce King. Oxford: Clarendon Press, 1996, 158.

9. Vasant A. Shahane. "What is Indian About Indian Sensibility." Dharwad: Karnataka University, 1986, 3.

10. Dieter Riemenschneider. "History and Individual in Salman Rushdie's *Midnight's Children* and Anita Desai's *Clear Light of Day*," *Kunapipi*, Vol. 6, No. 2, 1984, 58.

11. David W. Price. "Salman Rushdie's Use and Abuse of History in *Midnight's Children*," *Ariel*, Vol. 25, No. 2, 1994, 103.

12. Partha Chatterjee. *The Nation and Its Fragments*. Delhi: OUP, 1992, 227.

13. Chatterjee 224-25.

14. Chatterjee 224.

15. Richard Lannoy. *The Speaking Tree: A Study of Indian Culture and Society*. London: OUP, 1971, 289.

16. Mujeebuddin Syed. "*Midnight's Children* and Its Indian Contexts," *The Journal of Commonwealth Literature*, Vol. XXIX, No. 2, 1994, 101.

17. Wilson Harris. "Judgement and Dream" in *Imagined Commonwealths*, ed. T.J. Cribb. London: Macmillan, 1999, 56.

18. Mary Layoun. "The Strategy of Narrative Form," *Critical Exchange*, vol. 22 (Spring 1987), 40.

WORKS CITED

Ahmed, Aijaz. *In Theory*. Delhi: OUP, 1992.

Anderson, Benedict. *Imagined Communities: Reflections on the Origins and Spread of Nationalism*. London: Verso, 1983.

Boal, Augusto. *Theatre of the Oppressed*. New York, 1985.

Boehmer, E. *Colonial and Postcolonial Literature*. Delhi: OUP, 1995.

Freire, Paulo. *Pedagogy of the Oppressed*. New York, 1970.

Gandhi, Mahatma. *Hind Swaraj*. 1938, reprint, Navjivan Publishing House, Ahmedabad.

Gandhi, Leela. *Postcolonial Theory: A Critical Introduction*. Delhi: OUP, 1999.

Goonetilleke, D.C.R.A. *Salman Rushdie*. London: Macmillan, 1998.

Gugelberger, George M. "Decolonizing the Canon: Considerations of Third World Literature," *New Literary Theory*, 22, 1991.

Harlowe, Barbara. *Resistance Literature*. London, 1987.

Jameson, Fredric. "Third World Literature in the Era of Multinational Capitalism," Social Text, 15 (1986), 65-88.

Mishra, Vijay. "The Great Indian Epic and Peter Brook," in *Peter Brook and "The Mahabharata:" Critical Perspectives*, ed. David Williams. London: Routledge, 1991, 195-205.

Nazareth, Peter, *The Third World Writer: His Social Responsibility*. Nairobi, 1978.

Nehru, Jawahar Lal. *The Discovery of India*. London: Meridian Books Ltd., 1946.

——. *An Autobiography*. (1936), Delhi: OUP, 1989.

Renan, Ernest. "What is a Nation" (1982), in *Nation and Narration*, ed. Homi K. Bhabha. London: Routledge, 1990.

Rose, Jacqueline. *States of Fantasy*. Oxford: Clarendon Press, 1996.

Rushdie, Salman. *Midnight's Children*. (1981), New York: Avov.

——. "Outside the Whale," *Granta*, 11 (1984), 125-38.

——. "Rushdie Interview" in *Scripsi*, 3: 2/3 (1985), 107-26.

——. "*Midnight's Chidren* and *Shame*," *Kunapipi*, 7:1 (1985), 1-19.

——. "*Imaginary Homelands: Essays and Criticism 1981-1991*. London: Granta, 1991.

Rushdie, Salman. *The Moor's Last Sigh*. London: Jonathan Cape, 1995.

———. Rushdie's "*Midnight's Children*," in the *Guardian*, 15 March 1998.

Said, Edward. *Orientalism*. (1978), Harmondsworth: Penguin, 3rd ed., 1991.

Seth, Vikram. *A Suitable Boy*. New Delhi: Viking (Penguin India), 1993.

Sidhwa, Bapsi. "Third World, Our World," *The Massachusetts Review*. Winter, 88-89.

Singh, Jyotsna G. *Colonial Narrative/Cultural Dialogues*. London: Routledge, 1996.

5

Feminist Perspectives in Salman Rushdie's *Midnight's Children*

Ramesh Kumar Gupta

> "The situation of woman is that—she, a free and autonomous being like all creatures—nevertheless finds herself living in a world where men compel her to assume the status of the other."
>
> (Simone de Beauvoir: *The Second Sex*)

Kate Millett in "Sexual Politics" considers it the 'power-nexus.' Referring to Henry Miller's "Sexus," she writes of "a male assertion . of dominance over a weak, compliant, and rather unintelligent female. It is a case of sexual politics at the fundamental level of copulation.[1] In Lawrence's *Men and Women* Sheila Mcleod also illustrates this term 'power-nexus':

> Women's work has long been downgraded and devalued when compared to man's work, male muscular strength has been prized above the female capacity for physical endurance, men have been the owners of wealth and property, the wielders of authority, the holders of power, the achievers, the doers, the go-getters, while women have been barred from such apparently desirable positions or behaviours.[2]

In Rushdie's *Midnight's Children* Padma is the partner—partner not only for bed but for life too, a devoted nurse and above all a submissive soul to Saleem Sinai. Padma is a prey of masculine might. She is portrayed only in a descriptive manner by Saleem. There are other characters also that figure in the novel, have an unwholesome affinity among themselves. Rushdie himself assumes it to be "a book that discusses the relationships between history and private lives.[3] Dieter Reimenschneider also considers that *Midnight's Children*...is essentially concerned with man's quest for his identity."[4] D.W. Atkinson, a reputed observer, illustrates *Midnight's Children* as an autobiographical novel, projecting grandiosely the 'macro-reality' of national concerns as an extension of the 'macro-reality' of self."[5] Critics have discussed several aspects of the novel but there are a few critics who have discussed Padma. Uma Parameswaran remarks that Padma "is many things within the novel, and certainly deserves a full study."[6] In this paper, the study is concentrated on Padma, though it is felt that the sexist bias operates against nearly all women characters in the novel.

Padma is a prey of male chauvinistic society. She is depicted in the novel through her animal materiality. Saleem Sinai does not hesitate to refer to her as "Padma—our plump Padma...sulking magnificently (She can't read...Padma: strong, jolly, a consolation for my last days. But definitely a bitch-in-the-manger)" (*Midnight's Children*: 1982, 24). This explanation does not display her in a positive light and it is followed by a still more damaging hint: "Pamda snorts. Wrist smacks against forehead. 'Okay, starve starve, who cares two pice? Another louder, conclusive snort.... Thick of waist, somewhat hairy of forearm, she flounces, gesticulates, exists. Poor Padma (*ibidem.*, 24). Padma is compared to a bitch, she cajols, snorts; moves her hand up down up and so on. She is illiterate, ignorant and unpleasant as well. Saleem calls her 'plump,' 'thick of waist' and 'somewhat hairy forearm.' He again says Padma "really—truly was a witch?" (*ibid.*, 381). This indicates Saleem's repugnant attitude towards Padma.

Padma's works present her as a sheer stereotype. She is busy for Saleem. She cooks food for Saleem, prepares his bed, and after all becomes disappointed when she is ignored by him. Her works have no recognition and appreciation. Padma's honest devotion, simplicity and submissiveness have no meaning. Here, masculine power claims that man knows better. Padma is illiterate so she is far from the competences of reading and writing. But writing is Saleem's estate on which basis—time, history and politics are willingly monopolized by him, and cooking and making bed are not significant. Saleem appears as an order-giver whereas Padma a good maintainer. Saleem ever derides her for illiteracy and passivity. He evinces his hegemonic view by saying: "I attempt to educate her" (*ibid.*, 38). He states that he is quite aware of the people, politics, society and culture of India. Saleem, like Rushdie, depicts the socio-economic experience which keeps Padma an illiterate. This is the social-order which keeps the women uneducated here. This social-order explicates it as a case of sex-difference which is founded by male power in our Indian society. Only they have divided their roles and rights on the gender-difference. Cooking food, washing clothes, giving birth to children and nourishing them, making beds for husbands and waiting for them, nursing them are all women's trades and the rest are made for men. Man has *de facto*, power from the very beginning so he raises his own status to a high level and degrades woman's *etat*. After all, tout le monde knows that cooking food is no less intriguing than narrating history or writing autobiography.

The negative aspect of passionate desire is constructed around Padma for Saleem. As we see in the novel, Saleem does not fulfil Padma's carnal craving and any physical demand. Instead of satiating her, he claims that Padma is a mere sample of sensual raven. It implies that man is mighty on the sensual project as well. He elevates symbolic reference of Padma's sexual urge in a vulgar way. But after passing a long period, Saleem avows that he is no good in bed. Padma has been deceived into believing that Saleem must be physically fit. It is a turning point for Saleem to see her only as a bitch in ardour of youth. His manly might appears of no worth. Padma's requirements are emotional and psychic but it is refractory of Saleem to imply that she craves only for sex. Voluntarily, Padma demands to be his companion and it indicates that carnal desire is not the destination of her life. She would be fortunate if Saleem could give some good, loving, caring, touching and sympathetic moments to her. But Saleem has no inclination for it. This city—dweller Saleem has no time for this vulgar rustic girl. Her only defect or crime is that she has immolated herself at the altar of Saleem's love. It is Saleem's love that has trapped her. Therefore, she is in his custody and pines for his love. Padma says:

> So then I thought, how to go back to this man who will not love me and only does some foolish writing? (Forgive, Saleem baba, but I must tell it truly. And love, to us women, is the greatest thing of all). (*Ibid.*, 193)

Her submissive-soul is moaning out of Saleem's sense, sympathy and love. Here, one thing is to be noted that Padma is a Hindu woman and she loves a man who is a sterile Muslim widower. That inspite of all rough and tumble situations she decides to marry and stay with him is a clear indication of the devotional love. The novelist presents a statement through Saleem Sinai in support of Padma's pitiable plight *viz.*,

> Our Padma bibi, long-suffering tolerant consoling, is beginning to behave exactly like a traditional Indian wife. (And I, with my distances and self-absorption, like a husband?) Of late, in spite of my stoic fatalism about the spreading cracks, I have smelled, on Padma's breath, the dream of an alternative (but impossible) future; ignoring the implacable finalities of inner fissures, she has began to exude the bittersweet fragrance of hop-for-marriage. My dung-lotus, who remained impervious for so long to the sneer-lipped barbs hurled by our workforce of downy-forearmed women, who placed her cohabitation with me outside and above all codes of social propriety, has seemingly succumbed to a desire for legitimacy...in short, although she has not said a word on the subject, she is waiting for me to make an honest woman of her. The perfume of her sad hopefulness permeates her most innocently solicitous remarks. (*Ibid.*, 384-85)

She appears as though she has sold her whole life for the sake of his love. Saleem takes her as an object of use. He needs warmth of affection, care and food and she is supposed to provide his all requirements. But in return, Padma is treated as a 'nymphomaniac' by him. It is perplexing to justify Saleem's heartless, emotionless and surface notions to her: "I don't blame Padma." Saleem does not neglect Padma's presence. He cannot bear Padma's absences. He wants her and consequently takes her presence for granted, but then being a male he despises to show his urge. This duality presents his callousness. He degrades her, derides her, exploits her and still expects her to be loyal to him. In this circumstance it is Padma who loves him and is ever ready to digest his words. Padma says: "This love, mister, Padma is wailing for, it will drive a woman to craziness" (*Ibid.*, 193).

In this novel Padma is portrayed in terms more of gaps and absences than presences. Her absence depicts the critical background of her past, her family structure and her social status. She appears to be depicted only as a foot mat to Saleem the narrator, and is displayed to have only human concerns. She has no liberty, no existence and no identity. Her past and present along with family background are crushed out. Her identity is denied when Saleem talks of history or politics. "Padma began to cry: 'I never said I didn't believe, she wept.' Of course, every man must tell his story in his own true way; but..." (*Ibid.*, 211). She is discarded at every level of life. Saleem denies her but the readers have sympathy for Padma. Saleem goes three generations back to initiate his anecdote as, "you see, Padma: I have told this story before" (*Ibid.*, 365) and so narrates his tale that in place of knowing him, the readers will have to know a lot of lives, but he has no place for Padma to hold an opinion in his life. "Grieve for Saleem— who, orphaned and purified, deprived of the hundred daily pin-pricks of family life, which alone could deflate the great ballooning fantasy of history and bring it down to a more manageably human scale, had been pulled up by his roots to be flung unceremoniously across the years, fated to plunge memoryless into an adulthood whose every aspect grew daily more grotesque" (*Ibid.*, 345). Padma's past, present, parents and pleasure all are lost in Saleem's story.

Padma is depicted as the 'lotus-Goddess' in the novel. When she was small, she had been named after the lotus goddess by her mother, whose most common appellation amongst village folk is "The One Who Possesses Dung"

(*Ibid.*, 24). Perhaps, there is no contrast at all. In this regard the novelist presents Padma as one, "Who along with the Yaksa genii, who represent the sacred treasure of the earth, and the sacred rivers, Ganga-Yamuna-Saraswati, and the true goddess, is one of the Guardians of Life, beguiling and comforting mortal men while they pass through the dreamweb of Maya. Padma, the Lotus calyx, which grew out of Vishnu's navel, and from which Brahma himself was born; Padma the Source, the mother of Time!..." (*Ibid.*, 194-95). The characteristics of masculine power need to recompense man's real disgrace and exploitation of woman by doling out to her some supernatural, and bewildering space in which she is adored as a deity. This bewildering space is the notion of her sex. This imaginary space is an indication of legalizing her real exploitation continuously. The reference to Padma as the lotus goddess has no meaning to her, though she may consider it so, in that she is a willing dupe of the sex politics of India. Padma is Saleem's disdained other, utilizable, exploitable and submissive soul. Here, she is presented as a mere commodity of sex. She is not only a slave of Saleem but also a prey of illiteracy. The novelist presents this paradigm not only for Padma but also for the women in general. Robin Morgan proposes that the new feminist moral vision is in many ways analogous to the vision of reality offered by the new physics. She sees feminism as "crucial to the continuation of sentient life on this planet." It is the key to our survival and transformation. The reason she offers is that women have over the centuries developed an ethic that is appropriate to the world view that is emerging out of the new physics: they see in terms of relationship and in terms of environmental contexts. Moreover, women have been the custodians of human values for centuries. Their primary value is a reverence for life. This ethic must become the governing world ethic.[7]

Padma is considered a subject to male domination and she wishes to convert her name from Padma Mongril to Naseem Sinai. What Saleem expects, Padma does more for him. That is why she is amongst those who are men's women. Rushdie has illustrated Padma as a 'submissive soul' or 'agonised self' who acts according to her master's voice sans knowing it. She is not free to act according to her choice. She is evinced as a pathetic prey in Saleem's house. The readers of this novel do not regard her as an ideal in Indian ethos. Beauvoir set up a *de facto* trap whereby women are constantly faced with the threat of demission, or back-sliding in "being of female passivity."[8] The woman in this novel is certainly more aware of the injustice done to her by masculine power but habit makes her a willing detenu in this world of exploitation and injustice. Padma looks like a submissive soul that does not have courage to break a long relationship which has become purportless with no sense of companionship or partnership between gamete and gametes.

Thus, Rushdie's *Midnight's Children* has several qualities, but its gender-difference presents the submissive soul of the protagonist Padma and it appears despicable and incongruous to all who have faith in the similarity of sexes. She is a stereotype and over-duped figure of woman in a male-chauvinistic society. In this figure woman is marginalized, while man occupies ample right to dominate in the society.

NOTES AND REFERENCES

1. Kate Millett. "Sexual Politics" (1969; rpt., London: Rupert Hart-Davis, 1971), 6.

2. Sheila Mcleod. "The Passion to be Masculine," *Lawrence's Men and Women* (1985; rpt., London: Paladin Grafton Books, 1987), 18.

3. Malvika, Rajbans Sanghvi. "You Fight to Like Where You Live," *Indian Express Magazine*, March 20, 1983, V.

4. Dieter Reimenschneider. "History and Individual in Anita Desai's *Clear Light of Day* and Salman Rushdie's *Midnight's Children*," World Literature Written in English, 23 (1984), 196.

5. David W. Atkinson. *Abstracts of English Studies*, 27 (September 1984), 2293.

6. Uma Parameswaran. "Salman Rushdie in Indo-English Literature," *Journal of Indian Writing in English*, 12 (July 1984), 24.

7. Robin Morgan. *The Anatomy of Freedom: Feminism, Physics, and Global Politics* (New York: Doubleday, 1982), 282-83.

8. Helene Lamoure Eisenberg. "The Theme of Demission in the Works of Simone de Beauvoir" (Ph.D. Dissertation, University of California, Berkeley, 1978).

6

Dichotomy of Vision as Central Structural Motifs in *Midnight's Children* and *Shame*

SEEMA BHADURI

'The one thing that stays constant in the shifts between the dimensions in one's own consciouness....'

Rushdie, Grimus

Shame[1] was published one year after *Midnight's Children*[2] and the two narratives seem radically different from each other. Yet, the major themes and constructive principles of both these novels are the same. Not merely that; the two novels are mutually complementary, for each one of them emphasises by contrast, the formal integrity of the other.

The basic narrative technique in both the texts involves the treating of all things in terms of duality. This is Rushdie's way of dramatising the dichotomy of vision[3] which, as his protagonist Saleem finds in *Midnight's Children*, originated in the historical world-view that came to India with the colonialists. This dichotomy became, in both the novels, characteristic of all reality. Everything, since then, is found to be inherently dualistic, containing mutually contradictory characteristics. This theme of the dichotomy of vision leads to three other thematic propositions of equal importance to the two novels: That dualities inherent in all reality continue to multiply infinitely with changing human perspectives and developing awareness; that this multiplicity ebbs and dies away with decreasing awareness; that awareness flowers with time and only in a state of freedom. These propositions determine most of the narrative methods in both the novels.

and inconsistency. He perceives himself as ideologically under attack and his authoritarianism is tinged by his own religious and cultural marginality. He, therefore, constantly feels the need to masculinise himself to preserve his self-esteem and valourise aggression, achievement, control competition and power. In this context, an interesting study in comparison is Rabindranath Tagore's *Gora*³ where the hero adopts an ultra-Hindu fundamentalist posture to preserve his self-esteem in conditions of humiliating colonial rule. However, unlike Rabindranath, Rushdie seldom explores the real anguish or anxiety of the fascist in making or any possibility of his/her realisation of the unsoundness of ideologies professed and valourised. His fascists are unmitigated evil men and women with a touch of the comic and the grotesque about them. What is interesting is the range and variety of his fascist and shades of the fascist personality that abound in his works. Though his primary concern is with the fascist in the political sphere, politics in the subcontinent is inextricably mingled with religious fundamentalism and the authoritarian personality often enthusiastically espouses religious causes in his quest for total control of power. Equally interesting is the fascist in the domestic sphere; the patriarch or the matriarch who makes skilful use of socially sanctioned power positions to consolidate their hegemonic control. Science, technology or order created through reason and logic are some other weapons to exert control.

In his very first novel *Grimus,* the central character is middle European scientist with a past. This was to become trademark of the authoritarian personality to which Rushdie would return again and again. Perhaps Rushdie had Adorno's model in mind—the failed intellectual and the frustrated artist who becomes a perverted power crazy dictator. Grimus is the failed scientist and uprooted migrant, "...semi-Semitic prisoner of war...the destruction of his human dignity, of his belief in the whole of human race; the subsequent burrowing away, away from the world, into books and philosophies and mythologies, until these became his reality, since he had no regards for species he did not care what he did to them. They had done enough to him" (*Grimus* 243).

Grimus has remarkable similarities with the Christian God complete with his Other, the Devil or in this case, Deggle, whom he has expelled. The only difference between them is Grimus' technological superiority and not any intrinsic moral worth. Grimus has created the town of K (a parody of the garden of Eden?), where people are petrified into perfection and material satisfaction. Grimus wants to immortalise himself by choosing his exact double, Flapping Eagle. But Eagle refuses fusion, retains his identity while rejecting Grimus and reversing his aim—the preservation and perpetuation of calf Islands, where Eternity, the halting of time and mortality, have merely created a hell of unending patterns of thought and behaviour. While the world of Grimus is dissolving, Eagle is mating with Media—a confession that the supreme joy lies in unmaking the rigid framework of divine perfection. While questioning the order and perfection, which the dictator seeks to create, Rushdie also questions the intrinsic worth of the man who hides behind his creation. When discovered and confronted, Grimus appears to be extremely ordinary and unprepossessing, knitting on a chair. *Grimus*, after all, is an early, experimental novel, and the portrait of the dictator is abstract and theoretical.

The authoritarian personality really comes to life in *Midnight's Children*, where a real historical figure, Indira Gandhi, or the Widow as she is called in the novel and her protégees like son Sanjay and Major Shiva, weave patterns of dominance and control to lead people into the land of perpetual midnight. In the figure of the Widow, Rushdie combines the abstract fear of the fascist with the particular Indian (Hindu) anxiety about the ill-omened woman whose husband is dead and more specifically the fear of the castrating mother figure. The Widow chooses the Cow and the Calf symbol as her election symbol and literally unleashes a reign of terror with her forced sterilisation programme. The anxiety is expressed in Saleem's words, "But above all, the Widow.... How are we to understand my too-many women? As the multiple faces of Bharat Mata? Or as even more...as the dynamic aspect of maya, as cosmic energy, which is represented in the female organ?...they are all aspects of Devi, the goddess who is Shakti, who slew the buffalo-demon, who defeated the ogre Mahesh, who is Kali, Durga, Chandi, Chamunda, Uma, Sati and Parvati...and who, when active is coloured red?" (*Midnight's Children* 406).

In the Indian context, the fascist as a mother has a special significance as the Indian male's first model of the authoritarian personality is his mother. As Ashis Nandy notes, "In terms of organisation of personality, a number of studies suggest that the Indian lives in his inner world less with a feared father, than with a powerful, aggressive mother. Manifestly, he idealises her and sees her as the final repository of all nurture and motherliness. Underneath this are deep doubts about the stability of her nurture and the way she uses her powers to aggress. Contrarily, the father is seen as non-interfering, inefficacious, distant as a co-victim of a castrating mother. Not surprisingly, in most cases, it is the mother who serves the Indian as his ultimate model of authority, to be deified, admired or obeyed. In fact, his identification with her equips him with certain 'feminine' passive-aggressiveness as his latent fear of her underwrites his frequent use of femininity as a major symbol of violence, retribution and evil."[4]

What begins as a vague anxiety about a bad mother, soon deepens into horror, as the Widow resorts to forced sterilisation programmes and imposition of the infamous Emergency, "and suspension-of-civil rights, and censorship-of-the-press, and armoured-units-on-special-alert, and arrest-of-subversive-elements" (*Midnight's Children* 439). As a metaphoric midnight descends upon India, reality begins to resemble a nightmare—"Yes perhaps a nightmare; green and black the Widow's hair and clutching hand and children muff and little balls go flying green and black her hand is green her nails are black as black" (*Midnight's Children* 422).

Combining the ominous figure of the Widow whose husband is dead and the threatening mother who resembles fantastic figures like "dayans, jinns and bhoot"[5] Rushdie creates a fascist who is unique in literature. The study acquires special relevance in the year 2000, which mourns the twenty-fifth anniversary of the imposition of Emergency, one of the darkest chapters of Indian history, when all civil rights were suspended and all democratic norms abandoned. The figure of Shiva, one of the many midnight's children and a blind admirer of the Widow and her son Sanjay's dictatorial policies, is one of the many Rushdie's marginal men, trying to make sense of his deculturation, rootlessness and poverty by wholeheartedly supporting a fascist regime and valourising a kind of senseless machismo. In Shiva alone does Rushdie express some measure of anguish and dilemma and he is a fascist constantly torn apart by doubt regarding self-worth and self-esteem.

In *Shame,* there are two full-fledged figures, General Zia-ul-Haq and Zulfikar Ali Bhutto, only thinly veiled as Raza Hyder and Iskander Harappa.

The portrait of the fascist as a military dictator and religious fundamentalist is wonderfully done in the figure of Old Razor Guts or Reza Hyder. "Eleven years ago, he burst out of his bottle like an *Arabian Nights* goblin, and although he seemed at first, a small puny sort of demon, he instantly commenced to grow, until he was gigantic enough to be able to grab the whole of Pakistan by throat" (*Imaginary Homelands* 53). As Rushdie tells us in his essay entitled *Zia-ul-Haq, 17th August 1988,* "Pakistan under Zia [became] a nightmarish surreal land" where armaments were openly traded in the country's black market, police and military actively supported drug peddlers, where elections took place without political parties, where dictator imposed "his Islamisation programme...the ugliest possible face of faith." (*Imaginary Homelands* 53-54). In *Shame,* the fascist is also the religious leader who is not merely content to control people's bodies, but their minds. The narrator notes, "Autocratic regimes find it useful to espouse the rhetoric of faith, because people respect that language, are reluctant to oppose it. This is how religions shore up dictators; by encircling them with words of power, words which people are reluctant to see discredited, disenfranchised, mocked" (*Shame* 251). Raza therefore heeds the sayings of God and bans booze, censors all television programmes except theological lectures, strictly imposes praying five times a day, shoots down beggars, and muzzles any kind of opposition ruthlessly. But what makes fictional Raza Hyder's rule all the more nightmarish, is the constant demeaning of women, their constant shaming, which leads to the birth of violent beast Sufiya Zinoba. In *Shame,* the portrait of the fascist is nuanced by the inclusion of oppressive patriarchy. As Bilquis' father, who has been derisively named, Mahmoud the Woman says, "Woman...is there no end to the burdens this world is capable of bearing? Was there ever such a broad-backed and also such dirty word?" (*Shame* 62). In Raza's rigid patriarchal household, women act as instruments of oppression. Bilquis' anger and shame at giving birth to a female child and the neglect and oppression meted out to the retarded Sufiya Zinoba is only possible in a society where women are devalued at all levels of existence.

Iskander Harappa, the smart, western-educated, so-called upholder of democracy, is an equally old hand at silencing political opposition, unleashing a reign of terror and using women as playthings, flaunting the likes of Pinkie Aurangzeb in presence of his wife Rani Harappa. Ultimately, however, male authority in *Shame* is subverted and dictators rendered impotent, as women, defying all logic, appear as enormously powerful and destructive. Violence engenders violence and the culture of intolerance, oppression and senseless cruelty that Raza had perpetrated literally comes home to him as his daughter is metamorphosed into a beast that copulates with men and tears their heads off. The final irony is Raza's escape camouflaged in a woman's burqua (veil) and his brutal end at the hands of three old women, the three mothers of Omar Khyam Shakil. Iskander's fall is embroidered in Rani Harappa's exquisite shawl.

Haroun and the Sea of Stories has many similarities with his first book *Grimus* as both deal with abstract figures peopling imaginary lands. Again in both the tales, tyrants have their exact doubles, complicating and enriching the texture of the narrative. Mr. Sengupta, a clerk at the offices of the City Corporation, is the cause of a domestic tragedy in Haroun's house, as his mother runs away with him. Sengupta is as prosaic and unimaginative as Haroun's father is creative, making a living as he does, by telling stories. His lookalike, Khattam Shud, the feared dictator of Chup, "is the Arch-Enemy of all stories, even of language itself. He is the Prince of Silence and the Foe of Speech." (*Haroun and the Sea of Stories* 39). Both Khattam Shud and Sengupta ask a similar question "What's the use of stories that aren't even true?" In *Haroun and the Sea of Stories* Rushdie pits the dictator against the artist in an attempt to establish that the stories, though factually incorrect, are conceptually true and therefore intrinsically threatening to the dictator who wishes to control the bodies and minds of people. Khattam Shud is determined to dam up the very well-spring of stories. "'But why do you hate stories so much?' Haroun blurted, feeling stunned. 'Stories are fun.' 'The World, however, is not for fun,' Khattam Shud replied. 'The World is for controlling.' 'Which World?' Haroun made himself ask. 'Your world, my world, all worlds' came the reply. They are all there to be ruled. And inside every single story, inside every stream in the Ocean, there lies a world, a story world, that I cannot Rule at all. And that is the reason why" (*Haroun and the Sea of Stories* 161).

Rushdie goes on to show that stories do have real life consequences as Rashid's stories make Butto, the Dictator of Dull Valley, appear ridiculous to his subjects, leading ultimately to his downfall. It is obvious that Khattam Shud is Rushdie's tormenter, Ayatollah Khomeini. The fictional dictator is however easily foiled as he is crushed to death, in a cartoon-like fashion by the huge idol Bezaban breaking upon him.

In *The Moor's Last Sigh*, Rushdie again returns to the context of the subcontinent and a dictator who is an identifiable political figure. Raman Fielding, who gets his name because of a cricket crazy father, who hovered on the peripheries of Bombay Gymkhana and pleaded to be given, if not one batting or bowling, then at least one fielding, turns out to be a ferocious don, using religious fundamentalism to power his rise in the murky world of Indian politics. "Raman Fielding's name derived, according to legend, from a cricket-mad father, a street-wise Bombay ragamuffin who hung around the Bombay Gymkhana, pleading to be given a chance: 'Please, Babujis, you give this poor chokra one batting? One bowling only? Okay, okay-then *just one fielding?*'...the immortal C.K. Naidu, who recognised him from the old days at the Gymkhana and joked, 'So, my little just-one-fielding...you sure grew up to take some expert catches.' After that the fellow was always known as J.O. Fielding, and proudly accepted the name as his own" (*The Moor's Last Sigh* 230).

He has remarkable similarities with marginal men like Shiva, who rose from humble backgrounds to interact with the rich and mighty. The most obvious result is a deep-seated unease with aristrocats...an ambivalent desire to humiliate them and at the same time curry their favours. As a failed artist who could never rise above the level of a cartoonist, he is determined to lay down the axioms of good art guided by his so-called religious considerations. He promotes the sculptor, Uma Saraswati, as a true representative of "Hindu" and therefore Indian art and launches a hate campaign to denigrate Aurora's paintings, which according to him are anti-national.

Cricket like art becomes a site to be politicised and used for communal ends. "In his bizarre conception of cricket as a fundamentally communalist game, essentially Hindu but with its Hindu-ness constantly under threat from the country's other treacherous communities, lay the origins of his political philosophy, and the 'Mumbai's Axis' itself.... Thus uniting regional and religious nationalism in his potent, explosive new group.

Cricket, most individualistic of all team sports, ironically became the basis of the rigidly hierarchic, neo-Stalinist inner structures of 'Mumbai's Axis,' or M.A., as it quickly came to be known" (*The Moor's Last Sigh* 231).

Raman Fielding is able to gauge and successfully utilise the desire of urban Indians uprooted from their local or vernacular cultures to belong to a clear-cut, goal-oriented, unabashedly aggressive programme, that promises to crush all outsiders, religious or regional and lead the chosen on a path of prosperity and self pride.

"What was interesting was how much the city's blue-blood cared for Fielding.... The youngest, sleekest, hippest young cats in the urban jungle came to prowl in his Lalgaum grounds.... He was against unions, in favour of breaking strikes, against working women, in favour of Sati, against poverty and in favour of wealth. He was against 'immigrants' to the city, by which he meant all non-Marathi speakers, including those who had been born there, and in favour of its 'natural residents', which included Marathi-medium types who had just stepped off the bus.... He spoke of a golden age 'before the invasions' when good Hindu men and women could roam free. 'Now our freedom, our beloved nation, is buried beneath the things the invaders have built. This true nation is what we must reclaim from beneath the layers of alien empires'" (*The Moor's Last Sigh* 298-99).

Like Shiva, he valourises hard masculinity and brute strength—"He had a power drive rather than sex drive.... He preferred male company. There would be evenings when in company of a group of saffron-head-banded M.A. Youth Wingers he would institute a sort of macho, impromptu mini-Olympiad. There would be arm-wrestling and mat-wrestling, push up contest and living-room boxing bouts" (*The Moor's Last Sigh* 300).

Unlike Shiva, however, there are no redeeming touches to Fielding/Mainduck and he is presented as an unalloyed ogre who dies by the same sword, he had wielded when alive.

What is disturbing about Fielding's portrait is the increasing acceptability of such quick-fix solution vendors in the Indian polity and a growing support for a culture of violence and intolerance to any kind of asymmetry or deviation from the perceived norm. From a structural point of view, fascists constitute a counterpoint to the hybrid, translated men and women with infinitely varied shades to their identity, in Rushdie's novels. The insistent recurrence of fascists, is also a reminder of the havoc, pain and human suffering that can be wrecked in the name of nation, religion, ethnic group or region by men/women espousing rigid ideological positions.

NOTES

1. All fictional and non-fictional works of Salman Rushdie are noted in the text with appropriate page number(s). Details of editions cited are noted in Works Cited.

2. For a detailed analysis of the so-called "Rushdie Affair", refer to—

   • Ziauddin Sardar and Merryl Wyn Davies, *Distorted Imagination: Lessons from the Rushdie Affair* (London: Grey Seal, 1990), 144-58, 161-62.

   • Malise Ruthven, *A Satanic Affair* (London: Chatto and Windus, 1990).

   • Lisa Appiganesi and Sara Maitland, eds. *The Rushdie File* (London: ICA/Fourth Estate, 1989).

3. Rabindranath Tagore. *Gora*, in Rabindra-Rachanabali (Reprint, Calcutta: West Bengal Government, 1961). Vol. 9, 1-350. English tr. Anon. (Calcutta: Macmillan, 1924, reprint 1965).

4. Ashis Nandy, *At the Edge of Psychology—Essays in Politics and Culture* (New Delhi: OUP, 1980), 107.

5. Sudhir Kakar, *The Inner World: A Psycho-analyst's Study of Childhood and Society in India* (New Delhi: OUP, 1981), 96.

WORKS CITED

A. Rushdie, Salman: Fiction

Grimus. London: Vintage, 1996; first published in Great Britain by Victor Gollanz Ltd. in 1975.

Haroun and the Sea of Stories. London: Granta Books in association with the Penguin Group, 1991; first published by Granta Books in 1990.

Midnight's Children. London: Vintage, 1995; first published in Great Britain by Jonathan Cape in 1981.

The Moor's Last Sigh. London: Vintage, 1995; first published in Great Britain by Jonathan Cape in 1995.

Shame. London: Vintage; first published in Great Britain by Jonathan Cape in 1983.

B. Rushdie, Salman: Non-Fiction

Imaginary Homelands; Essays and Criticism, 1981-1991. London: Granta Books in association with the Penguin Group, 1992; first published by Granta Books in 1991.

C. Others

- Appiganesi Lisa and Maitland Sara, eds. *The Rushdie File.* London: ICA/Fourth Estate, 1989.

- Fletcher, D.M. ed. *Reading Rushdie: Perspectives on the Fiction of Salman Rushdie.* Amsterdam: Rodopi, Cross/Cultures 16, 1994.

- Kakar, Sudhir. *The Inner World: A Psycho-analytic Study of Childhood and Society in India.* New Delhi: OUP, 1981, first published by OUP in 1978.

- Nandy, Ashis. *At the Edge of Psychology—Essays in Politics and Culture.* New Delhi: OUP, 1980.

- ——; *Return from Exile—Alternative Sciences, Illegitimacy of Nationalism, the Savage Freud.* New Delhi: OUP, 1998.

- ——; Trivedy, Shikha; Mayaram, Shail; Yagnik, Achyut. *Creating a Nationality: The Ramjanambhumi Movement and Fear of the Self.* New Delhi: OUP, 1998, first published in 1995.

- Ruthven, Malise. *A Satanic Affair.* London: Chatto and Windus, 1990.

- Sardar, Ziauddin and Wyn Davies, Merryl. *Distorted Imagination: Lessons from the Rushdie Affair,* London: Grey Seal, 1990.

- Tagore, Rabindranath. *Gora* in *Rabindra-Rachanabali,* reprint Calcutta, West Bengal Government, 1961, Vol. 9, 1-350. English tr. Anon. Calcutta: Macmillan, 1924, reprint 1965.

10

Negating the 'Old Stable Ego of the Character': Multiple Identity in the Novels of Rushdie

MICHAEL HENSEN

In Salman Rushdie's latest novel *The Ground Beneath Her Feet* (1999) the first-person narrator makes the following statement about the identity of one of the protagonists:

> To her last day, I could always see in her the skittish, disintegrated creature she'd been when she first came to us, looking as if she might run away again at any moment. What a piece of jetsam she was then, what a casualty! Literally selfless, her personality smashed, like a mirror, by the fist of her life. Her name, her mother and family, her sense of place and home and safety and belonging and being loved, her belief in the future, all these things had been pulled out from under her, like a rug. She was floating in a void, denatured, dehistoried, clawing at the shapelessness, trying to make some sort of mark.... She was a rag-bag of selves, torn fragments of people she might have become. Some days she sat crumpled in a corner like a string-cut puppet, and when she jerked into life you never knew who would be there, in her skin. (Rushdie 1999: 121-22)

From this statement it immediately becomes clear that "the old stable ego of the character" (Lawrence, qtd. in Gorra 1994: 655) and therefore also the traditional approach of the self as being developed out of family or place is to be dismissed when analysing Rushdie's novels. In order to show how

Rushdie perceives identity, a closer look at an approach to identity by the social sciences seems to be particularly rewarding as it differentiates between personal and social identity.

1. Personal and Social Identity

Personal identity, according to the psycho-sociologist Erik Erikson, is an individual's "subjective sense of a continuous existence and a coherent memory" (Erikson 1968: 61). According to the sociologist Peter Wagner, who elaborates on Erikson's theory, this definition communicates several messages. Firstly, this means that identity is highly subjective and can only be gained through a self-reflexive process (cf. also Kamm *et al.* 1994: 12), secondly, that this process is used to develop a continuous existence, although there might have been breaks and faults in one's life, and thirdly, that the individual's mind tries to generate a coherent view of itself, i.e. tries to identify past events as part of its own identity (Wagner 1998: 45).

Social identity, by contrast, is the identification of one individual with the other, be it a small group, a religious community, or a nation (Wagner 1998: 45). What is important, however, is the dialectical relationship between these two aspects of the term "identity." Social identity, on the one hand, necessitates the existence of several people's personal identities targeting the same objective. On the other hand, personal identity can often only be comprehended in terms of denial or acceptance of collective or cultural values, indicating that there is a gap, or call it *différance* in the Derridaean sense, between society or parts of it and the individual self (Wagner 1998: 46). This difference means that in order to keep one's identity one will have to interpret oneself constantly, and by doing so one is constructing one's own identity. If identity is regarded as a construct (cf. Assmann & Friese 1998: 12-13; Motz 2000; Wagner 1998: 63-65), then the notion of easy coherence in life and continuity of the self is deceptive as there will always be ruptures and discontinuities. This means that in the postmodern or poststructuralist sense, identity is to be regarded as an adaptable and thus unstable and fluid entity, and that identity is the product of continuing exchange and endless negotiations (Assmann & Friese 1998: 12).

2. Deconstruction of Identity in the Traditional Sense

2.1 *Parents and Family/Family Name*

The family (especially the parents) has been traditionally seen as central to a person's identity. In most of Rushdie's novels, however, the protagonists do not really know who their parents are, or if they do, they deliberately choose not to accept this insight.

Saleem Sinai in *Midnight's Children* makes the reader believe that his parents are Ahmed and Amina Sinai, a wealthy Indian couple, and he also describes in great detail their life and experiences. In the middle of the novel it becomes clear, though, that after the delivery, the nurse Mary Pereira swapped two babies, so that Saleem is actually not the midnight's child Saleem Sinai, but the baby he was swapped for, i.e. Shiva. This means that Saleem would be the child of the poor busker Wee Willie Winkie and his wife Vanita. But nine months before the delivery Vanita had sexual intercourse with the Englishman William Methwold, so that Saleem turns out to be of Anglo-Indian descent (Rushdie 1982: 118). This is something he constantly denies and he rather chooses to believe that Ahmed and Amina still are his parents (Rushdie 1982: 118). Thus, Saleem deliberately makes up, or constructs, his parents and his descent, later also naming other potential parents: the nurse Mary Pereira and Nadir Khan (Rushdie 1982: 127), Mr. Schaapsteeker (Rushdie 1982: 148-49) or Picture Singh (Rushdie 1982: 378).

More or less the same holds true for *The Ground Beneath Her Feet* where the protagonist and rockstar Vina Apsara can be seen as having five different parents. She is the American-born child of a Greek-American mother and an Indian father. After the divorce her mother marries again, this time an American by origin, but the second marriage drives the mother mad and being utterly desperate she kills herself and the rest of the family, sparing only her daughter, who is then transferred to other American relatives at the West Coast. But they, having run out of money, contact the girl's Indian relatives who promise to take her as their daughter. As a result of having been treated badly there she flees and finally arrives at the house of the first-person narrator, whose parents, Ameer and Vivvy are the last parents to accept her as their child.

This multiplication of parentage in *Midnight's Children*, as well as in *The Ground Beneath Her Feet*, is seemingly nonsensical but works in the way of a reverse pattern: by naming too many parents none seems to be plausible so that both protagonists can be viewed as being in a state of orphanhood and displacement. Accordingly, Juan-Navarro contends that Rushdie's protagonists lack a symbolic centre (Juan-Navarro 1993: 269), which is also underlined by the fact that Saleem is constantly referring to a "hole in the centre of me" (e.g. Rushdie 1982: 192). Nevertheless, both protagonists state that they can maintain their identity and they do so by constructing a coherent view of themselves.[1]

This is also true of Moraes Zogoiby, the protagonist of *The Moor's Last Sigh* who is disinherited by his parents and finally kicked out of the parental home:

> I stumbled through them [the gates], giddy, disoriented, lost. I was nobody, nothing. Nothing I had ever known was of use, nor could I any longer say that I knew it. I had been emptied, invalidated; I was, to use a hoary but suddenly fitting epithet, ruined. I had fallen from grace, and the horror of it shattered the universe, like a mirror. I felt as though I, too, had shattered; as if I were falling to earth, not as myself, but as a thousand and one fragmented images of myself, trapped in shards of glass. (Rushdie 1995: 278-79)

Despite this shattered vision Moraes has of himself at this moment, he later seems to be able to collect himself and claim to have found his true self without needing his parents any more: "I need no longer be what ancestry, breeding and misfortune had decreed, but could enter, at long last, into myself—my true self" (Rushdie 1995: 295). Read on another level, this implies that Moraes' move from his former hybrid identity towards a simplistic and easily determinable one, mirrors the state India is in.[2] At the end of the novel, however,

Moraes makes a plea for a broad concept of identity as he conjures up his predecessors from all around the globe: King Arthur, Barbarossa, Finn MacCool and the Worm Ouroboros (cf. Rushdie 1995: 433).

The Ground Beneath Her Feet offers yet another aspect to the point that identity may also be seen as independent of one's family background. Apart from calling five different couples her parents, Vina Apsara, in keeping with the traditions of the music business, makes up her own name: 'Vina' for an Indian musical instrument and also for being morphologically close to 'Divina,' and 'Apsara' who, according to Hindu myth, is a beautiful nymph who is consorting with other mythical beings skilled in music and who is constantly tempting men (cf. Knappert 1991: 52). In the course of the novel it turns out that both parts of her chosen name will prove right for her behaviour: she is not only skilled in all music matters but also in seducing and consuming men. From this it seems possible that by constructing one's name one can also construct one's identity.

2.2 *Place and Home*

Another element of the traditional view of identity is that a person's character is determined by the environment she or he grows up or lives in. This is questioned in Rushdie's novels because most of the protagonists are migrants who do not see place as a feature by which a person's character is moulded.

In *Grimus* the orphaned protagonist, Flapping Eagle, is forced to leave his tribe and wander aimlessly around the world, and in *Midnight's Children* Saleem travels the whole Indian subcontinent physically as well as by his telepathic powers. *The Satanic Verses* offers another angle when the Indian protagonists, Saladin Chamcha and Gibreel Farishta, migrate to England, go back to India in the end, and in between dream themselves into different times and places. Moraes Zogoiby in *The Moor's Last Sigh* travels India as well as Spain, and his father changes his appearance and character according to whether he deals with the world overneath or underneath, i.e. with the underworld (Rushdie 1995: 179-80).

What all these novels also have in common regarding the notion of place is firstly, that one can strike one's roots in any culture, and secondly, that the culture one is brought up in cannot be easily pinned down either. For example, the Cochin-born Moraes is of Jewish-Christian-Muslim descent and Vina Apsara is of Greek-Indian-American origin. This means that the notion of a single, fixed identity cannot easily be ascribed to place and cultural roots because these in themselves already are the product of diversity and intermingling (cf. also Bhabha 1994: 35).

3. Identity and Hybridity

Most of Rushdie's protagonists are migrants, of their own will—migrants who have to construct their personal identity in relation to the often entirely different social identity around them. They have chosen a specific country and culture, and then have the possibility to make themselves at home there and to put down roots. This is something Umeed Merchant, the Indian-born first-person narrator of *The Ground Beneath Her Feet*, senses when he looks at his new house in New York:

> So this is what they feel like, I thought: roots. Not the ones we're born with, can't help having, but the ones we put down in our own chosen soil, the you could say radical selections we make for ourselves. (Rushdie 1999: 414)

The question is, however, whether the migrant chooses, or selects to put down roots after all. This may not be the case, taking into account that his or her sense of personal identity might deviate considerably from the (assumed and actual) cultural identities of the appointed destination. What the migrant, usually being a member of a minority, senses is the difference and the tension between him or herself and the Other, and it is up to the migrant how to deal with it. The two extremes possible are either identification with or denial of cultural values.

This theme is developed in *The Satanic Verses*. Whereas the Indian Gibreel Farishta tries to hold on to a consistent idea of selfhood deciding not to adapt to English society, his fellow countryman Saladin Chamcha chooses to do just that. In the course of the novel Gibreel is rewarded, represented by his obtaining a halo (Rushdie 1992: 142) and passing his bad breath on to Saladin (Rushdie 1992: 133), who is being punished for having selected adaptation: he grows horns (Rushdie 1992: 141) and finally also a hoof. The narrator comments on the migrant status of Gibreel and Saladin:

> Should we even say that these are two fundamentally different *types* of self? Might we not agree that Gibreel,...— has wished to remain, to a large degree, *continuous*—that is, joined to and arising from his past;...so that his is still a self which, for our present purposes, we may describe as true...whereas Saladin Chamcha is a creature of *selected* discontinuities, a *willing* re-invention; his *preferred* revolt against history being what makes him, in our chosen idiom, 'false'?...—While Gibreel, to follow the logic of our established terminology, is to be considered 'good' by virtue of *wishing to remain*, for all his vicissitudes, at bottom an untranslated man.—But, and again but: this sounds, does it not, dangerously like an intentionalist fallacy?—Such distinctions, resting as they must on an idea of the self as being (ideally) his vicissitudes, at bottom an untranslated man—homogeneous, non-hybrid, 'pure,'—an utterly fantastic notion!—cannot, must not, suffice. (Rushdie 1992: 427)

This differentiation between good and evil with regard to the migrant's position towards adaptability is not only verbally deconstructed by the narrator. Later, back in India, Gibreel's problem of sulphurous halitosis returns with a vengeance on him, and he loses his girl-friend and his job before finally committing suicide (Rushdie 1992: 546), whereas Saladin is reconciled with his father, inherits his wealth and reunites with his girl-friend Zeeny Vakil (Rushdie 1992: 547).

Migrants on their quest for identity in their chosen new home can compare their identity with that of the others, and some of the migrants (Saladin, for example) might be able to translate themselves culturally. If they choose to do so, they will have to form their identity in the tension between the already known and the new culture. Thus, their identities become hybrid, meaning that their selves will be "composed of different or incongruous elements of heterogeneous sources" (*OED*). The term hybridity has its origins in the 19th-century biological theory, denoting the crossing of two different species (Young 1995: 12). Later, especially in colonial times, the term was used pejoratively for half-breeds, but in the broader sense the term nowadays alludes to the contact between two or more cultures, between the self and the Other (Bhabha 1994: 35; Fludernik 1998b: 11-12). The relationship between these two is dialectical, it is an irreconcilable contradiction and a difference that can never be solved, but one cannot be without the other either. This tension is what Bhabha terms "the third space" (Bhabha in an interview with Rutherford 1990: 211; Bhabha 1994: 37) and he uses this notion to "deconstruct the boundary between the self and other" (Fludernik 1998a: 51). This space between cultures is the one in which migrants move and out of which they will have to develop their personal identity. This idea of migrants' identities is exactly what most of Rushdie's novels elaborate on (cf. also Goetsch 1997: 143). In his essay "Imaginary Homelands"—the term itself being an alternative image for the third space—Rushdie subsequently talks about migrants' identities:

> Our identity is at once plural and partial. Sometimes we feel that we straddle two cultures; at other times that we fall between two stools. But, however ambiguous and shifting this ground may be, it is not an infertile territory for the writer to occupy. (Rushdie 1991: 15)

What the migrant can gain from his oscillation between the two (or more) cultures is a newness which can only be achieved by bringing together two seemingly incompatible positions. And this is also the answer to one of the narrator's central questions in *The Satanic Verses*: "How does newness come into the world?" (e.g. Rushdie 1992: 8). By breaking up dichotomies, by bringing together two dissimilar views, by joining the self with the Other.

It has to be stated, however, that migrants may also face serious problems and eventually even the loss of parts of their identity. Problems will inevitably arise if the majority puts pressure on the migrant, and the results of oppression are vividly depicted in Saladin's brutal arrest by several immigration officers (Rushdie 1992: 157-64). And by gaining something new, undoubtedly something old has to be left behind. This, for example, is powerfully outlined by the frequent references to incidents taking place in airplanes, a metaphor for crossing Bhabha's third space, in Rushdie's novels:

> In *The Satanic Verses* Saladin and Gibreel fall out of an exploding aircraft towards England, the fall symbolising their fall from grace as well as the fall of Lucifer,[3] and some of their transformations already start during their fall. In *The Moor's Last Sigh* Moraes boards an airplane and notices that his old understanding of his personal identity will probably not work any more.

You will see that I entered an unfamiliar state of mind. The place, language, people and customs I knew had all been removed from me by the simple act of boarding this flying vehicle; and these, for most of us, are the four anchors of the soul (Rushdie 1995: 383).[4]

And finally in *The Ground Beneath Her Feet* Ormus, the lover and future husband of Vina Apsara, "sheds his old skin...like a snake" (Rushdie 1999: 250) when flying from India towards London. Strikingly, the whole chapter dedicated to the flight is termed "Membrane," suggesting that all migrant travellers, by having to penetrate this membrane, can only save some parts of their identity and thus have to leave back some other parts:

> ...detached from the indifferent earth, he feels a certain resistance in the air. Something fighting back against the aircraft's forward movement. As if there's a stretchy translucent membrane across the sky, an ectoplasmic barrier, a Wall.... But it's so springy, this invisible restriction, it keeps pushing the airplane back, boeing!, boeing!, until at last the *Mayflower* breaks through, it's through! Sunlight bounces off the wing into his bleary eye. And as he passes that unseen frontier he sees the tear in the sky,.... He

intuits that every bone in his body is being irradiated by something pouring through the sky-rip, a mutation is occurring at the level of the cell, of the gene, of the particle. The person who arrives won't be the one who left, or not quite (Rushdie 1999: 253).[5]

This also compares with the notion of the migrant's (cultural) translation. The term translation, as Rushdie states, etymologically comes from the Latin word for 'bearing across':

> Having been borne across the world, we [migrants] are translated men. It is normally supposed that something always gets lost in translation; I cling, obstinately, to the notion that something can also be gained. (Rushdie 1991: 17)

4. Conclusion

It has become clear that almost all of Rushdie's novels suggest that an individual can never restrain from being influenced by cultural identity. Therefore, it is not surprising that Moraes speaks about "a self without walls" (Rushdie 1995: 288) and finally even draws the parallel between 14th-century multi-ethnic Granada and its Alhambra and the "need for flowing together, for putting an end to frontiers, for the dropping of the boundaries of the self" (Rushdie 1995: 433). Saleem Sinai, too, alludes to the notion of hybrid identity when he says:

> O eternal opposition of inside and outside! Because, a human being, inside himself, is anything but a whole, anything but homogeneous; all kinds of everywhichthing are jumbled up inside him, and he is one person one minute and another person the next. (Rushdie 1982: 236-37)

His later approach towards defining his personal identity can succeed only by relating the self to the environment.

> Who what am I? My answer: I am the sum total of everything that went before me, of all I have been seen done, of everything done-to-me. I am everyone everything whose being-in-the-world affected was affected by mine. I am anything that happens after I have gone which would not have happened if I had not come.... I repeat for the last time: to understand me, you'll have to swallow a world (Rushdie 1982: 383).

Other terms that frequently come up in Rushdie's novels are impurity, intermingling, transformation, mongrelization, mélange, hotchpotch, pastiche and finally palimpsest: What Rushdie has to say about *The Satanic Verses* thus certainly holds true for most of his novels.

The Satanic Verses celebrates hybridity, impurity, intermingling, the transformation that comes of new and unexpected combinations of human beings, cultures, ideas, politics, movies, songs. It rejoices in mongrelization and fears the absolutism of the Pure. Mélange, hotchpotch, a bit of this and a bit of that is how newness enters the world (Rushdie 1991: 394).

All these terms show that in Rushdie's novels identity is not a unitary entity but rather a fragment, not stable but fluid, not single but multiple, not coherent or continuous but hybrid. This does not mean that an individual cannot think himself or herself as coherent. One has to accept, however, certain discontinuities and ruptures in one's biography.

Thus, personal identity has to be seen as a perpetual process of negotiations with oneself and one's environment, which is very much in line with Zygmunt Bauman's statement on postmodern identity-building: "'identity,' though ostensibly a noun, behaves like a verb, albeit a strange one to be sure: it appears only in the future tense" (Bauman 1995: 82). Accordingly, Salman Rushdie goes beyond the theoretical approach outlined in the beginning: today identity arises out of cross-border and cross-continental exchange.

NOTES

1. In the case of Saleem Sinai this coherence is mainly achieved by the act of writing: "I must work fast, faster than Scheherazade, if I am to end up meaning—yes, meaning—something" (Rushdie 1982: 9) whereas Vina Apsara achieves this goal by singing. Thus, they both construct their identities by means of creating pieces of art, i.e. cultural constructs, and enhance the constructedness of their identity.

2. In this passage India's pluralistic society is severely threatened by semi-fictional Hindu fundamentalists (cf. Rushdie 1995: 290ff).

3. The carrier is named Bostan (Rushdie 1992: 4) after one of the Gardens of Eden (cf. also Aravamudan 1989: 8).

4. In this context Schülting's view of Moraes as being "the most hybrid of characters" in the novel holds true as he "possesses not two, but multiple identities, or, as he says, none at all" (Schülting 1998: 248-49).

5. In the context of this chapter it would also be possible to speak of 'cultural osmosis,' denoting that the contact between cultures is based on negotiation and the process of mutual give and take within the third space.

WORKS CITED

Aravamudan, Srinivas. "'Being God's Postman is no Fun, Yaar:' Salman Rushdie's *The Satanic Verses.*" *Diacritics: A Review of Contemporary Criticism*, 1989, 19.2. 3-20.

Assmann, Aleida and Heidrun Friese. "Einleitung." *Identitäten*. Ed. Aleida Assmann and Heidrun Friese. Frankfurt/Main: Suhrkamp, 1998, 11-23.

Bauman, Zygmunt. *Life in Fragments: Essays in Postmodern Morality*. Oxford: Blackwell, 1995.

Bhabha, Homi K. *The Location of Culture*. London: Routledge, 1994.

Erikson, Erik H. "Identity, Psychosocial." *International Encyclopedia of the Social Sciences*, Bk. 7. Ed. David L. Sills. London: Macmillan, 1968.

Fludernik, Monika. "The Constitution of Hybridity: Postcolonial Interventions." *Hybridity and Postcolonialism: Twentieth-Century Indian Literature*. Ed. Monika Fludernik. Tübingen: Stauffenburg, 1998a, 19-54.

——. "Introduction." *Hybridity and Postcolonialism: Twentieth-Century Indian Literature*. Ed. Monika Fludernik. Tübingen: Stauffenburg, 1998b, 9-18.

Goetsch, Paul. "Funktionen von Hybridität in der postkolonialen Theorie." *Literatur in Wissenschaft und Unterricht*, 1997, 30.2: 135-45.

Gorra, Michael. "Rudyard Kipling to Salman Rushdie: Imperialism to Postcolonialism." *The Columbia History of the British Novel*. Ed. John Richett. New York: Columbia UP, 1994, 631-57.

Juan-Navarro, Santiago. "The Dialogic Imagination of Salman Rushdie and Carlos Fuentes: National Allegories and the Scene of Writing in *Midnight's Children* and *Cristobal Nonato.*" *Neohelicon: Acta Comparationis Litterarum Universarum*, 1993, 20.2: 257-11.

Kamm, Jürgen, Norbert Schaffeld and Marion Spies. *Spuren der Identitätssuche in zeitgenössischen Literaturen.* Trier: WVT, 1994.

Knappert, Jan. *Indian Mythology: An Encyclopedia of Myth and Legend.* London: Aquarian Press, 1991.

Motz, Wolfram. *Die Konstruktion von Identität im schottischen Roman während der Ära des britischen Konservatismus 1979-1997.* Frankfurt/Main: Lang, 2000.

Rushdie, Salman. *Grimus.* London: Vintage, 1996 (1975).

———. *The Ground Beneath Her Feet: A Novel.* New York: Henry Holt, 1999.

———. "Imaginary Homelands." *Imaginary Homelands: Essays and Criticism 1981-1991.* Ed. Salman Rushdie. Harmondsworth: Penguin, 1991, 9-21.

———. *Midnight's Children.* London: Macmillan, 1982 (1981).

———. *The Moor's Last Sigh.* London: Cape, 1995.

———. *The Satanic Verses.* Dover (Del.): The Consortium, 1992 (1988).

Rutherford, Jonathan. "Interview with Homi Bhabha: The Third Space." *Identity: Community, Culture, Difference.* Ed. Jonathan Rutherford. London: Lawrence and Wishart, 1990, 207-21.

Schülting, Sabine. "Peeling off History in Salman Rushdie's *The Moor's Last Sigh.*" *Hybridity and Postcolonialism: Twentieth-Century Indian Literature.* Ed. Monika Fludernik. Tübingen: Stauffenburg, 1998, 239-60.

Wagner, Peter. "Fest-Stellungen. Beobachtungen zur sozial-wissenschaftlichen Diskussion über Identität." *Identitäten.* Ed. Aleida Assmann and Heidrun Friese. Frankfurt/Main: Suhrkamp, 1998, 44-72.

Young, Robert J.C. *Colonial Desire: Hybridity in Theory, Culture and Race.* London: Routledge, 1995.

11

Versions of the Postcolonial: Carnival, Masquerade and Grotesque Realism as Aspects of Rushdie's World

BLAIR MAHONEY

> In its multivalent oppositional play, carnival refuses to surrender the critical and cultural tools of the dominant class, and in this sense, carnival can be seen above all as a site of insurgency, and not merely withdrawal.
>
> —Mary Russo (218).

The novels of Salman Rushdie, especially *The Satanic Verses*, display a number of recurring elements: shifting and hybrid identities, the dislocation of the migrant, the dangers of essentialism and fixity, and the subversive carnivalesque elements of migrant subcultures. Mikhail Bakhtin's work on the transgressive nature of carnival and masquerade provides the tools to best explain the picture of postcolonial hybrid subjectivity that Rushdie depicts in his novels.

In his novels, Rushdie constructs versions of postcolonial subjectivity and the nation which break free of essentialist and monolithic thinking and which are based instead, on ideas of hybridity and multiplicity. He does this by depicting characters whose identities are shifting and multiple, who don a variety of masks without necessarily using them to conceal essential identities. The migrant is the perfect figure to illustrate this conception of multiple, shifting identity, for the migrant belongs in one sense everywhere and in another sense nowhere. Rushdie shows that a nation such as Great Britain is not as homogeneous as some of its inhabitants might like to think. The British Empire has come home, has imploded, bringing with it diverse, heterogeneous elements as migrants from the so-called "margins" converge on the so-called "centre." Some of these elements can be assimilated into the mainstream, but there always remains something unassimilable, an unreconcilable part that resists all efforts to suppress difference and contributes to the multiplicity of self and nation.

In contrast to the prevailing view that the postmodern fragmented subject is inimical to the prospect of political agency, Rushdie's novels demonstrate that a fixed and unitary identity is not necessary for the postcolonial subject to achieve agency and bring about political change. Indeed, Rushdie's hybrid and multiple characters are in many ways able to bring about more political change than are unchanging and static characters. It is through hybridity that newness and change enter the political world.

Postcolonial Carnival

Carnival is presented by Bakhtin as a world of topsy-turvy, of heteroglot exuberance, of ceaseless overrunning and excess where all is mixed, hybrid, ritually degraded and defiled.

—Stallybrass and White (8).

In the opening pages of *Rabelais and his World*, Bakhtin draws a distinction between two different types of worlds that existed in medieval Europe: one public and official, the other based on unofficial forms and outside the sphere of influence of Church and State. This latter world engaged in rituals of inversion that parodied and ridiculed those of the official world:

All these forms of protocol and ritual based on laughter and consecrated by tradition existed in all the countries of medieval Europe; they were sharply distinct from the serious official, ecclesiastical, feudal, and political cult forms and ceremonials. They offered a completely different, nonofficial, extraecclesiastical and extrapolitical aspect of the world, of man, and of human relations; they built a second world and a second life outside officialdom. (Bakhtin 5-6)

When Saladin Chamcha, in *The Satanic Verses*, returns to England after surviving the explosion of the plane by which he was travelling, it is a very different England to the one he left. He discovers a split between official and nonofficial worlds very similar to that described by Bakhtin.

In *The Satanic Verses*, the characters of Saladin Chamcha and Gibreel Farishta explore the range of carnivalesque options. The novel shows the split between official and nonofficial in the scenes of the riots that originate in the vicinity of Club Hot Wax. These riots express a popular uprising of those immigrant underclasses that feel they are being victimised by the police and the official authorities. Indeed, Saladin himself is the recipient of police brutality. The vicious beating he receives at the hand of the policemen could not have occurred in the official England that he once believed in; the official England is more like "that Sussex of rewards and fairies which every schoolboy knew" (SV 158). The police are very much a part of the official world, however, acting as the representatives of those who wield power.

This official role of the police is evident in the riot scenes which Rushdie describes using the terminology of television. The camera is often perceived as a neutral medium that merely presents the facts, but Rushdie shows that it is able to be manipulated and is a component of the official world, the world of order:

—Cut.—A man lit by a sun-gun speaks rapidly into a microphone. Behind him there is a disorderment of shadows. But between the reporter and the disordered shadow-lands there stands a wall: men in riot helmets, carrying shields.... A camera is a thing easily broken or purloined; its fragility makes it fastidious. A camera requires law, order, the thin blue line. Seeking to preserve itself, it remains behind the shielding wall, observing the shadow-lands from afar, and of course from above: that is, it chooses sides. (SV 454-55)

The camera looks down from above, that is, from the official world, onto the nonofficial world of the rioters. It is shielded from the nonofficial world by the line of policemen, and is representative of order, presenting the nonofficial world as a place of shadows and disorder. The positioning of the camera and reporter in the light of the sun guns associates Europeans (the media and the police) with light and reason and Africans and Asians (the rioters) with disorder and lawlessness. *The Satanic Verses* has introduced a racial element into the official and nonofficial worlds described by Bakhtin.

In *The Satanic Verses* the existing hierarchy mercilessly discriminates against the nonofficial immigrant culture which exists in London. Those immigrants, with their different religions and beliefs, are not compatible with "the existing religious, political, and moral values" of the official world (*SV* 9). They must turn instead to the nonofficial world of the carnivalesque, which Bakhtin describes as celebrating:

> temporary liberation from the prevailing truth and from the established order; it marked the suspension of all hierarchical rank, privileges, norms, and prohibitions. Carnival was the true feast of time, the feast of becoming, change, and renewal. It was hostile to all that was immortalized and completed. (Bakhtin 10)

The carnivalesque, then, is concerned with what Rushdie calls bringing newness into the world, with bringing about change in the existing order. Bakhtin also points out, however, that this liberation is only temporary.

One of the major criticisms of the carnival as a theoretical construct is that its transgressive power is licensed by the authorities, making it an outlet for radical urges to be harmlessly expelled. Peter Stallybrass and Allon White, for example, state that "[m]ost politically thoughtful commentators wonder, like Eagleton, whether the 'licensed release' of carnival is not simply a form of social control of the low by the high and therefore serves the interests of that very official culture which it apparently opposes" (Stallybrass & White 13).[1] Stallybrass and White go on, however, to claim that carnival is not completely ineffective in bringing about political and social change. When combined with a strong political agenda and a high level of friction in the community, it can bring about real change. They write, "for long periods carnival may be a stable and cyclical ritual with no noticeable politically transformative effects but that, given the presence of sharpened political antagonism, it may often act as *catalyst* and *site of actual and symbolic struggle*" (Stallybrass & White 14), and they observe that "it is in fact striking how frequently violent social clashes apparently 'coincided' with carnival" (Stallybrass & White 14). This coincidence between carnival and violent social clash occurs in *The Satanic Verses* when the riots, which bear many features of Bakhtin's carnival, erupt as a reaction against the racism of the English police. The regular rituals of inversion which take place in Club Hot Wax are relatively harmless expressions of displeasure towards the establishment, and as such are allowed to continue, but when these same sentiments meet with the catalyst of police brutality and the death in custody of a prominent figure in the community, they result in riots that have real potential to cause damage to the establishment. Action is taken, therefore, by those in power to try to prevent this more serious outpouring of carnivalesque practices.[2]

In one of the prominent carnivalesque scenes in *The Satanic Verses*, at Club Hot Wax, the crowd, predominantly immigrants, call out the name of the authority figure whose wax effigy they wish to see melted in a gigantic microwave oven:

> Attendants move toward the tableau of hate-figures, pounce upon the night's sacrificial offering, the one most often selected, if truth be told; at least three times a week. Her permawaved coiffure, her pearls, her suit of blue. *Maggie-maggie-maggie*, bays the crowd. *Burn-burn-burn*. The doll,—the *guy*,—is strapped into the Hot Seat. Pinkwalla throws the switch. And O how prettily she melts, from the inside out, crumpling into formlessness. Then she is a puddle, and the crowd sighs its ecstasy: *done*. "The fire this time," Pinkwalla tells them. Music regains the night. (*SV* 293)

Here, we see Bakhtin's ritual of transgression taking place in the unofficial underground world of the immigrants, who have suffered more than most due to the policies of the Conservative British government.[3] They select the figure of the Prime Minister to perform a comic uncrowning and humiliation of the supreme authority figure in the country. The events at Club Hot Wax are an inversion of the official ritual that takes place on November 5, when an effigy of Guy Fawkes, one of the rebels who tried to blow up the English parliament, is burnt. Rushdie alludes to this in the above passage when he refers to the effigy of Thatcher as a guy. In the official celebration a person who attempted to transgress the authority of the State is humiliated, but in the Hot Wax ritual it is the authority figure that is subjected to the melting that corresponds to Bakhtin's comic uncrowning.

The melting of the effigy is a carnivalesque celebration, and as such provides a "temporary liberation from the prevailing truth and from the established order," and a "suspension of all hierarchical rank, privileges, norms, and prohibitions" (Bakhtin 10). In Club Hot Wax, the patrons are temporarily out of the reach of racist taunts, police harassment and oppressive government policies. There all rank is suspended and they can invert the power relations between the Prime Minister and themselves, exercising their power over her image and exacting their symbolic revenge. The Club Hot Wax ritual corresponds closely to Bakhtin's description of medieval carnival and its rituals and symbols:

> We find here a characteristic logic, the peculiar logic of the "inside out" (à l'envers), of the "turnabout," of a continual shifting from top to bottom, from front to rear, of numerous parodies and travesties, humiliations, profanations, comic crownings and uncrownings. A second life, a second world of folk culture is thus constructed; it is to a certain extent a parody of the extracarnival life, a "world inside out." (Bakhtin 11)

The wax effigies are parodic representations of authority figures made to undergo a ritual humiliation. The comic uncrowning takes place in a microwave oven which melts them from the "inside out," exemplifying the logic of the inside out, whereby hierarchies are inverted and power relations altered for a temporary period. Such an inversion requires, of course, an acceptance of the existing categories, and a recognition that hierarchies of power exist between them. The carnival aims for social change of some sort, however, for, as Bakhtin says, it "was the true feast of time, the feast of becoming, change, and renewal" (Bakhtin 10).

Rushdie, in *The Satanic Verses*, tries to answer the question, "How does newness come into the world?" (*SV* 8), and the opening pages of the novel are replete with images of rebirth and change. The change that the novel is working towards is not simply an inversion of existing hierarchies such as we see occurring in Club Hot Wax; it involves moving through these binary oppositions to a new and hybrid conception of identity and culture. Rushdie provides an example of simplistic and destructive carnivalesque inversion in the novel when Gibreel Farishta imagines himself to be (and perhaps really is, by the novel's uncertain logic) the Archangel Gibreel, come to wreak vengeance on the godless English. In a scene that reverses the traditional relationship between coloniser and colonised, he imagines himself to be the one in the position of power, and even quotes Frantz Fanon on the desire of the colonised subject to invert the hierarchy in which he or she is trapped:

> He would show them—yes!—his *power*.—These powerless English!—Did they not think their history would return to haunt them?—"The native is an oppressed person whose permanent dream is to become the persecutor" (Fanon). English women no longer bound him; the conspiracy stood exposed!—Then away with all fogs. He would make this land anew. He was the Archangel, Gibreel.—*And I'm back!* (*SV* 353)

Gibreel here espouses a kind of philosophical absolutism in which he stands for absolute good and the English for absolute evil. He has reversed the hierarchy of colonialism and claims to see the true nature of the world: a world which does not allow for shades of meaning.

The theme of the destructive nature of such absolutism recurs throughout *The Satanic Verses* and closely ties in with the inversion of hierarchies. Such inversions reinscribe terms such as coloniser and colonised, confirming them as fixed categories. The only change that results is the perception of which term is superior. Such purity of ideals, and the taking up of the position of absolute adversary to some other absolute is shown to be ultimately ruinous in the cases of Tavleen the hijacker and Hind of Jahilia, as well as in Gibreel's case. Homi Bhabha's reading of Fanon emphasises the need to move beyond the absolutism that is required in the process of inverting the hierarchy and celebrating that which was formerly derided:

> Fanon recognises the crucial importance, for subordinated peoples, of asserting their indigenous cultural traditions and retrieving their repressed histories. But he is far too aware of the dangers of the fixity and fetishism of identities within the calcification of colonial cultures to recommend that "roots" be struck in the celebratory romance of the past or by homogenising the history of the present. (Bhabha 1994: 9)

The passage sheds light on the fragment of Fanon that is quoted by Gibreel, for it shows that although fixed origins and identity are, to some extent, understandable desires for the colonised subject, they can also be dangerous, as can the uncritical reversal of the power relations between the oppressor and the oppressed. As Bhabha and Rushdie indicate, it is more productive to accept fragmentation and diversity and to move past the binary oppositions altogether, toward an ideal that is predicated upon compromise and alliances that bridge difference.

The Satanic Verses and the Grotesque

> In shattering the mirror of representation, and its range of western bourgeois social and psychic "identifications," the spectacle of colonial fantasy sets itself up as an uncanny "double." Its terrifying figures—savages, grotesques, mimic men—reveal things so profoundly familiar to the West that it cannot bear to remember them.
>
> —Homi Bhabha (1984: 119-20).

One of the principle features of the carnival is what Bakhtin labels "grotesque realism." He describes the grotesque body as an image for the larger community, a community that continuously expands and is bound up in cycles of birth and rebirth, change and renewal: "The material bodily principle is contained not in the biological individual, not in the bourgeois ego, but in the people, a people who are continually growing and renewed. This is why all that is bodily becomes grandiose, exaggerated, immeasurable" (Bakhtin 19). As Bakhtin explains it, the image of the grotesque body is an unsettled one, continually in process and, due to the metamorphoses it experiences, connected with the multiple and hybrid identities written about by Rushdie. It thus has an uncertain relation to time, refusing to remain static and consistent for any significant period. Bakhtin also points out the ambivalence of the image: "The grotesque image," he writes:

> reflects a phenomenon in transformation, an as yet unfinished metamorphosis, of death and birth, growth and becoming. The relation to time is one determining trait of the grotesque image. The other indispensable trait is ambivalence. For in this image we find both poles of transformation, the old and the new, the dying and the procreating, the beginning and the end of the metamorphosis. (Bakhtin 24)

The ambivalence Bakhtin describes here is an important feature of grotesque realism and carnivalesque images in general. This ambivalence indicates that the images are not in themselves transgressive; they may be transgressive images but they carry no political force unless there is some motivation behind them—unless, as Stallybrass and White point out, the carnival is combined with concrete grievances and antagonism (Stallybrass & White 14). The ambivalence of grotesque realism and masquerade is due to their invocation of certain practices and institutions in order to undercut them; in order to arrive at the new they must first invoke the old. These invocations of the old mean operating within the existing system and being implicated in the very things that are being subverted.

The extent to which Bakhtin's description of the elements of grotesque realism coincides with the discourses of racism is quite remarkable, and illuminates in particular the incident in *The Satanic Verses* in which Saladin is transformed into a grotesque devil figure. Bakhtin considers the elements of grotesque realism, connected as they are with processes of change and renewal, to be positive, and this is how I have been treating them thus far: as positive ways to subvert the status quo and bring about change. The specific elements of grotesque realism which Bakhtin enumerates, though, are often used in negative racist stereotypes. For example, Bakhtin writes:

> The body discloses its essence as a principle of growth which exceeds its own limits only in copulation, pregnancy, childbirth, the throes of death, eating, drinking, or defecation. This is the ever unfinished, ever creating body, the link in the chain of genetic development, or more correctly speaking, two links shown at the point where they enter into each other. (Bakhtin 26)

In racist discourse, people of colour are frequently referred to as being grotesque in just this manner, as being primarily sexual, unclean, and forever reproducing. Bakhtin applies his analysis to the medieval poor in the novels of Rabelais, and such representations have also been applied to the underclasses, characterising them as a vast, squalid rabble. Bakhtin, nevertheless, sees these grotesque elements as positive forces for change instead of the degrading features of the downtrodden. In a similar fashion, Rushdie reclaims the negative images that have been applied to people of colour and uses them to mobilise resistance to the very racist discourses from which they come. The catalyst for the reclamation of negative images in *The Satanic Verses* is Saladin Chamcha, an Indian resident of England who becomes transformed into a grotesque, devilish creature.

Sometimes the differences between cultures can seem enormous, and Rushdie dramatises this perception of the gulf between cultures in his portrayal of the mutation of Saladin Chamcha into the horrific figure of racist fantasies and fears. Reflecting on his transformed, goatish, and Satanic form

Saladin says to himself, "The grotesque has me, as before the quotidian had me, in its thrall" (260). The grotesque works in two main ways in *The Satanic Verses*: as a literalisation of racist images of people of colour, and as a symbol of change and becoming: a potent force that can be harnessed and used to overthrow oppression.

Firstly, the grotesque figure that Saladin has become is the perfect object for the fear and loathing with which the racist views the immigrant of colour in Britain. When Saladin is arrested for being an illegal immigrant and is thrown into a police van he notices the changes that he appears to have undergone:

> His thighs had grown uncommonly wide and powerful as well as hairy. Below the knee the hairiness came to a halt, and his legs narrowed into tough, bony, almost fleshless calves, terminating in a pair of shiny, cloven hoofs, such as one might find on any billy-goat. Saladin was also taken aback by the sight of his phallus, greatly enlarged and embarrassingly erect, an organ that he had the greatest difficulty in acknowledging as his own. (*SV* 157)

Chamcha is puzzled that the policemen in the van take his bizarre transformation completely within their stride, but were he more aware of the racism of his adopted country he would not be so surprised at their acceptance of his Satanic appearance. His animal-like appearance and his visible strength and sexual potency literally reproduce their racist conceptions. He is a creature both to be feared and to be ridiculed. His difference is greatly exaggerated as he is completely transformed into the Other that bears no resemblance to "normal" human beings such as the white, middle-class, male policemen. These racist policemen also perceive people of colour as dirty and lacking in personal hygiene, and Saladin fulfils their expectations when he leaves goat pellets on the floor of the van, leading one of the policemen to remark, "You're all the same. Can't expect animals to observe civilized standards. Eh?" (*SV* 159).

Rushdie makes a number of points here, and the prominent one concerns racist stereotypes. The policeman makes the comment that "they" (immigrants) are all the same, and by so doing fixes a single identity onto a large and heterogeneous group of people. The problem is not so much that he is wrong to see all immigrants as dirty and ignorant of British standards of cleanliness, but more that he is wrong to both identify all immigrants as the same and to fix that identity onto them, precluding any possibility of diversity or of change. It is not that the policemen mistakenly see immigrants as unclean, strong, and virile, but rather that immigrants, like Britons of European heritage, are a diverse group of people who cannot be categorised in such a rigid and destructive manner. And to go even further, it would not matter even if the stereotypes were generally true, for each person deserves to be treated individually, not just as a member of a larger group defined by one attribute such as race or sex. Rushdie is not trying to say that racists are wrong in saying that all immigrants are bad because "in fact" all immigrants are good; he is, instead, portraying characters who are both good and bad at the same time.

The racist attitudes held by the policemen and others are responsible for the transformation of Saladin into a grotesque, satanic creature. When Saladin is taken to a prison hospital full of creatures similar to himself, and asks another inmate why they are like this, he gets the answer, "They describe us .... That's all. They have the power of description, and we succumb to the pictures they construct" (168). By describing him and other immigrants in this degrading manner, the policemen have turned them into precisely what it is that they fear and despise. Following the logic of the novel, in which ideas become reality, Saladin encounters a woman at the hospital who literalises the common racist idea that immigrants breed at a rapid rate and their aim is to take over the country:

> he heard a woman grunting and shrieking, at what sounded like the end of a painful labour; followed by the yowling of a new-born baby. However, the woman's cries did not subside when the baby's began; if anything, they redoubled in their intensity, and perhaps fifteen minutes later Chamcha distinctly heard a second infant's voice joining the first.

> Still the woman's birth-agony refused to end, and at intervals ranging from fifteen to thirty minutes for what seemed like an endless time she continued to add new babies to the already improbable numbers marching, like conquering armies, from her womb. (*SV* 166)

Such literalisations as this undermine the racist ideas on which they are based by showing just how ludicrous they are. Rushdie has pushed the racist fear or fantasy to grotesque extremes here, and, while debilitating for the woman who must endure such constant agony, the fantasy also threatens the racists who conceived it, with the image of the conquering armies marching out of her womb. Those racists use grotesque realism as an oppressive construct in the form of racist stereotypes, but oppressed groups can reclaim the grotesque images as a site of resistance, turning the images against their creators.

Bakhtin has identified what he calls the "essential principle" of grotesque realism as degradation, "that is, the lowering of all that is high, spiritual, ideal, abstract; it is a transfer to the material level, to the sphere of earth and body in their indissoluble unity" (Bakhtin 19-20). Saladin's transformation into a goat-like creature involves precisely this physicalising of the abstract. He represents Satan, brought down to earth in physical form, and he embodies abstract racist conceptions of immigrants. Bakhtin does not, however, conceptualise degradation as the entirely negative process of racist oppression, but instead sees it as containing the potential for positive change and renewal. Like the images of rebirth which proliferate in the opening chapter of *The Satanic Verses*, he speaks of new beginnings and birth arising out of death:

> To degrade is to bury, to sow, and to kill simultaneously, in order to bring forth something more and better.... Degradation digs a bodily grave for a new birth; it has not only a destructive, negative aspect, but also a regenerating one. To degrade an object does not imply merely hurling it into the void of nonexistence, into absolute destruction, but to hurl it down to the reproductive lower stratum, the zone in which conception and a new birth take place.

> Grotesque realism knows no other lower level; it is the fruitful earth and womb. It is always conceiving. (*SV* 21)

Bakhtin answers Rushdie's question "[h]ow does newness come into the world?" (Bakhtin 8) by suggesting that it emerges out of the processes of death and degradation. He sees the grotesque body as a symbol of change with its continual transformations and focus on the processes of life, such as birth, death, eating, drinking, and defecation. He takes those images which form a large part of racist constructions and looks for their positive and transformative elements. This reclamation of predominantly negative images plays an important part in *The Satanic Verses*.

The first instance of such a reclamation in the novel occurs when the prophet in the Jahilia section of the novel takes the name Mahound:

> Here he is neither Mahomet nor MoeHammered; has adopted, instead, the demon-tag the farangis hung around his neck. To turn insults into strengths, whigs, tories, Blacks all chose to wear with pride the names they were given in scorn; likewise, our mountain-climbing, prophet-motivated solitary is to be the medieval baby-frightener, the Devil's synonym: Mahound. (*SV* 93)

Similarly, Jumpy Joshi reclaims, in a poem he has written, Enoch Powell's notorious racist "River of Blood" metaphor, hoping to turn it into something that can be used to oppose racism instead of support it (*SV* 186). And later in the novel Uhuru Simba reclaims the role of the "uppity nigger" who is out to cause trouble and promote change (*SV* 414). The most powerful image of reclamation in the novel, however, is of that very grotesque and racist image that Saladin has come to literally embody. The oppressed underclass start to mobilise around this image, seeing in the grotesque body, as did Bakhtin, a potent force for change and rebirth. Children begin wearing rubber devil-horns and Saladin's satanic form starts to appear on banners at political demonstrations. Once more, the language of reclamation is used as Mishal explains to Saladin the reasons for his popularity: "you're a hero. I mean, people can really identify with you. It's an image white society has rejected for so long that we can really take it, you know, occupy it, inhabit it, reclaim it and make it our own" (*SV* 286-87). There is an ambivalence here that harks back to my earlier mention of the way that the racist images of the grotesque are products of both fantasy and fear. As with the image of the woman continually giving birth to the "conquering armies," the grotesque creature that Saladin has become is both degrading and frightening. He is, as his fellow inmate in the prison hospital tells him, a product of racist conceptions and descriptions, yet those very descriptions have transformed him into a being that has the power to strike back against them. Mishal observes that the other immigrants can really identify with him, and they can unite under him in order to fight against the common experience of oppression of which he is a symbol. By refusing to observe the diversity and individual skills and attributes of the various ethnic minorities and instead lumping them all together, the racists have unwittingly also provided them with the unity that they require in order to strike back against oppression. The various groups have united on the issue of racial oppression, forging a common identity that has in some ways also been thrust upon them, and have worked together despite their many differences to try and achieve change in this one area.[4]

The Satanic Verses and Masquerade

The notion that man has a body distinct from his soul, is to be expunged; this I shall do, by printing in the infernal method, by corrosives, which in Hell are salutary and medicinal, melting apparent surfaces away, and displaying the infinite which was hid.

—William Blake, *The Marriage of Heaven and Hell*

Bakhtin has written of masquerade, another of the important elements of the carnival, that the mask is:

the most complex theme of folk culture. The mask is connected with the joy of change and reincarnation, with gay relativity and with the merry negation of uniformity and similarity; *it rejects conformity to oneself.* The mask is related to transition, metamorphoses, the violation of natural boundaries, to mockery and familiar nicknames. It contains the playful element of life; it is based on a peculiar interrelation of reality and image, characteristic of the most ancient rituals and spectacles. (Bakhtin 39-40, my emphasis)

As with grotesque realism, and indeed all elements of carnival, Bakhtin perceives masquerade to be intricately bound up with notions of change and rebirth. This is because when one puts on a mask one is reborn as a new person, to an extent; one identity has been changed for another, or, to look at it another way, one identity has been hidden beneath another.[5] The above quotation, however, proposes a radical notion of difference. Bakhtin suggests that the masquerade emphasises difference not between self and other, but difference *within* the self; masquerade exposes the self as multiple rather than as a unified whole, because masquerading as a different self reveals the presence of more than one self in the same body. Like grotesque realism, masquerade embodies the act of transformation, indeed, Bakhtin says that "[i]t reveals the essence of the grotesque" (Bakhtin 40). More specifically, the use of masks results in "such manifestations as parodies, caricatures, grimaces, eccentric postures, and comic gestures" (Bakhtin 40). Just as the grotesque body is continually metamorphosing into different selves, so the masquerader changes masks and dons new selves. Bakhtin sees the use of masks as symbolic of reincarnation; they alter people's identities, allowing them to be "reborn" as new people. The masquerade contributes to the play of difference and the feeling of uncertainty that is a central feature of carnival in its unsettling of official certainties and fixity.

The principal participants in *The Satanic Verses* are, by their very professions, party to the practice of putting on masks, as both Gibreel and Saladin are actors. Gibreel is a superstar of Indian cinema, and specialises in portraying deities in movies that are known as "theologicals." James Harrison has pointed out that a particularly profound metamorphosis must take place when an actor portrays a deity, and at the start of his long career Gibreel often had to don masks in order to play Hanuman the monkey god or Ganesh the elephant-headed god (Harrison 91). Saladin, too, is no stranger to masks in his career as an actor in England. Mostly forced to do voice-overs due to his unfortunate handicap of having the wrong skin colour to appear on television (as his manager Hal Valance informs him, ads "research better" without people "of the tinted persuasion" in them), Saladin becomes the "man of a thousand voices," able to use his voice as a mask, changing voices to take on different identities while he remains unseen. Later, he lands a leading role on a television programme called "The Aliens Show," but he has to remain unseen, once more, hidden beneath a latex suit.[6]

The effect that masquerade has when bringing together apparently incompatible notions or selves can also be used to good effect by the migrant who wishes to subvert existing structures. The narrator of *The Satanic Verses*, for example, muses on the effectiveness of masquerade as a strategy of resistance for the migrant:

> A man who sets out to make himself up is taking on the Creator's role, according to one way of seeing things; he's unnatural, a blasphemer, an abomination of abominations. From another angle, you could see pathos in him, heroism in his struggle, in his willingness to risk: not all mutants survive. Or, consider him sociopolitically: most migrants learn, and can become disguises. Our own false descriptions to counter the falsehoods invented about us, concealing for reasons of security our secret selves. (*SV* 49)

The narrator presents a number of views on masquerade here, all coming from different angles. The first comes from a religious perspective that is steeped in purity and the sovereignty of the whole and individual self. Such a perspective cannot allow either the blasphemy of usurping the role of the Creator or the heresy of the hybrid or multiple self. The second perspective considers masquerade to be a risky business, a heroic struggle against oppression. The last, and I think most interesting viewpoint, sees masquerade as a process of resistance against the racism that many migrants encounter. In order to counter the false and damaging descriptions of those such as the police officers who beat up Saladin, the migrant is forced to come up with alternative identities, identities which need not be any closer to an objective "truth" than those perpetuated by racists, but which protect the migrant from further abuse. Indeed, the suggestion is made that it may even be desirable to construct "false" identities in order to protect a self or selves that the migrant wishes to remain secret. In this way, the young Saladin at boarding school learns to masquerade as a way of becoming accepted:

> he began to act, to find masks that these fellows would recognize, paleface masks, clown-masks, until he fooled them into thinking he was *okay*, he was *people-like-us*. He fooled them the way a sensitive human being can persuade gorillas to accept him into their family, to fondle and caress and stuff bananas in his mouth. (*SV* 43)

His masquerade is a survival technique, and principally involves suppressing differences and imitating features of the group to which he wants to belong. Rushdie's description of Saladin's masquerade involves an ironic twist in that he likens the imitator to a human gaining acceptance from a group of gorillas, despite Saladin being the one who is doing the "aping."

Rushdie explores the existence of a secret, possibly essential and unchanging, self beneath the masks worn by the migrant in a number of ways in *The Satanic Verses*. Changez Chamchawala sees his son desperately trying to become an Englishman and does not approve of this rejection of an Indian self that he perceives as essential and unchanging. In a letter to Saladin he associates such a masquerade with Satan, who Saladin ironically comes to resemble in a transformation that is not of his willing:

> "A man untrue to himself becomes a two-legged lie, and such beasts are Shaitan's best work," he wrote, and also, in a more sentimental vein: "I have your soul kept safe, my son, here in this walnut-tree. The devil has only your body. When you are free of him, return and claim your immortal spirit. It flourishes in the garden." (*SV* 48)

This view, with its separation of body and soul, of depths and surfaces, echoes that of Zeeny Vakil, who urges Saladin to drop his masquerade and become Indian once more, something that he is not prepared to do, even though his body also seems to be trying to persuade him as his accent starts to slip, and he starts to speak once more in a "Bombay lilt." At other times, however, she sees not an essential Indian self beneath his masks, but a void, the "terrible vacuum" that Bakhtin associated with the Romantic mask: "when you aren't doing funny voices or acting grand, and when you forget people are watching, you look just like a blank. You know? An empty slate, nobody home" (*SV* 61). Pamela, too, sees this absence at Saladin's core: "I could see the centre of you, that question so frightful that you had to protect it with all that posturing certainty. That empty space" (*SV* 183). Saladin himself reinforces this view of identity as a series of masks beneath which there is not an essential being but rather an absence of being when he reflects on the meaning of an oft-used cliché:

> *I'm not myself*, he thought as a faint-fluttering feeling began in the vicinity of his heart. But what does that mean, anyway, he added bitterly. After all, "les acteurs ne sont pas des gens," as the great ham Frederick had explained in *Les Enfants du Paradis*. Masks beneath masks until suddenly the bare bloodless skull. (*SV* 34)

By saying "I'm not myself," Saladin implicitly compares a certain outward self-image to an internal model from which it differs. When he says that, though, he suddenly realises the literal truth of this statement, as he has no essential self he can locate to which he can compare his outward mask. In his idea of himself he consists entirely of masks, which, when he removes them, expose the absence that Zeeny and Pamela have caught glimpses of. Rushdie suggests here that, by denying his Indian side, Saladin empties himself, becoming the absence perceived by Zeeny and Pamela. He becomes complete at the end of the novel only when he accepts his Indian selves as part of his multiple and hybrid construction.

The question of the nature of the self is addressed explicitly by Muhammad Sufyan, the proprietor of the Shaandaar Café, as he ponders the nature of Saladin's metamorphosis. He comments that the "Question of mutability of the essence of the self...has long been subject of profound debate" (*SV* 276), and characterises the debate as being divided between the views of Lucretius and those of Ovid. According to Lucretius, "Whatever by its changing goes out of its frontiers...that thing...by doing so brings immediate death to its old self" (*SV* 276). This means that we have no essential being and that when one identity is replaced by another, the old one is irrevocably lost. Saladin, before his transformation, inclines toward this view when he considers that he has put his old self behind him and replaced it with his new, English identity. Working against this, however, his voice starts to slip on his return to India, and his old self seems to be struggling out from behind his mask. Muhammad Sufyan himself subscribes to the Ovidian conception of identity which allows for an immortal essence: "As yielding wax...is stamped with new designs and changes shape and seems not still the same, yet is indeed the same, even so our souls...are still the same forever, but adopt In their migrations ever-varying forms" (*SV* 276-77).

While Saladin appears to fail in his quest to discard his Indian identity in favour of an English one, he decides to throw himself into his new Satanic identity, and become that totally, even as he sees he has no choice in the matter:

> He chose Lucretius over Ovid. The inconstant soul, the mutability of everything, das Ich, every last speck.... He would enter into his new self; *he would become what he had become*: loud, stenchy, hideous, outsize, grotesque, inhuman, powerful. (*SV* 288-89)

Saladin therefore internalises his external condition, becoming the identity that has been thrust upon him. He embraces his grotesque new identity, and, although he detests his appearance, he still recognises the powerful possibilities it contains.

Overall, the novel, like Muhammad Sufyan, tends towards the Ovidian rather than the Lucretian conception of identity. In the bizarre opening scene of the novel, Gibreel, as he falls towards England out of an exploded plane, sings a song which aptly summarises Ovid's view of an eternal essence as the basis of identity:

> "O, my shoes are Japanese," Gibreel sang, translating the old song into English in semi-conscious deference to the uprushing host-nation, "These trousers English, if you please. On my head, red Russian hat; my heart's Indian for all that." (*SV* 5)

Underneath the multicultural exterior lies an essence, a heart, a soul, that retains his Indian identity. The clothes, and outward appearance and behaviour in general, may define a person in some way, but they cannot alter every part of the individual, something remains unaltered, just as wax melted and shaped into a different form is still wax. This is the message that we get from Saladin's trip back to India where he detects his old identity trying to creep back: "Watch out, Chamcha, look out for your shadow. That black fellow creeping up behind" (*SV* 53). His voice betrays him, slipping back to a 'Bombay lilt' he thought he had left behind, and after the plane crash he finds his face has also lost the rigidity that he has cultivated and returned to its old cherubic state. As much as he tries to rid himself of this self, the novel seems to suggest, it keeps on coming back. This reaches a climax when he visits his father on his deathbed and reaches a reconciliation with him. As he sat next to his father:

> Saladin felt hourly closer to many old, rejected selves, many alternative Saladins—or rather Salahuddins—which had split off from himself as he made his various life choices, but which had apparently continued to exist, perhaps in the parallel universes of quantum theory. (*SV* 523)

Once more his old self, or, as is stated here, selves, are coming back to haunt him. Instead of continuing to reject these selves, however, he starts feeling closer to them, coming to terms with himself (himselves) at the same time he comes to terms with his father. These old selves he identifies with his old name, Salahuddin, a name he had rejected in his quest to become what he perceived as English, and a name which he now comes to embrace once more. Names are another outward indicator of possible identifications, and Saladin changed his to become more accepted in England. Now, however, he changes back to Salahuddin to identify once more as an Indian. The passage quoted suggests a continuing essence of some sort that has persisted despite the changes that Saladin has made in his life. That essence, however, grows and multiplies with him and does not remain fixed and unchanging. It is a hybrid rather than a pure essence, and consists of all the identities that he has previously adopted. Rushdie suggests in the conclusion of the novel that one can never leave behind one's past, and, at the same time, that one's past is not a solid and fixed object but a varied and multiple essence.

The conclusion of *The Satanic Verses* ties up the carnivalesque elements in the novel. Saladin has transcended the crude inversions of carnival exemplified by Gibreel and his adversarial attitude. He no longer rejects his Indian side and has reached a space of negotiation between his English and Indian elements where newness can emerge. That newness is a hybrid combination of all the selves, English and Indian, that he has constructed. He no longer has the physically grotesque features that were a result of racist conceptions, but he retains the spirit of grotesque realism described by Bakhtin. He remains a body in process, continually changing and evolving into something new, dying and being reborn as he transforms from a cynical mimic into a loving son and reclaims his heritage. He also keeps the spirit of masquerade, changing masks and creating hybrid identities as he does so. The resolution he reaches means that he no longer rejects his Indian selves, meaning that he now embodies the essence of the palimpsest. Whereas before he hid a void beneath his multiple masks because he abjured those Indian parts of his identity, he now has identity written over identity, the new selves overlaying the old and creating rich, new hybrid identities. This is the ideal of hybrid identity proposed by Rushdie.

NOTES

1. In a similar vein, Diane Price Herndl writes, "Bakhtin's carnival, however much it exposed the arbitrariness of the

social relations of power, remained an event allowed (if not sanctioned) by institutional authority, which served that institution by providing an outlet for the oppressed to prevent any *real* insurrection. It was an artificial subversion of hierarchies which prevented any organized question of them" (Herndl 19-20).

2. Rushdie observes the connection between the carnivalesque practice of masquerade and political revolution in *The Jaguar Smile* when he sees the masks covering the walls of the Nicaraguan Vice-President, the novelist Sergio Ramírez: "During the insurrection, Sandinista guerillas often went into action wearing masks of pink mesh with simple faces painted on them. These masks, too, originated in folk-dance. One night I went to see a ballet based on the country's popular dances, and saw that one of the ballerinas was wearing a pink mask. The mask's associations with the revolution had grown so strong that it transformed her, in my eyes at least, into something wondrously strange: not a masked dancer, but a guerrilla in a tutu" (*JS* 25-6). The popular dance is another carnivalesque practice that combines with the mask to form an image of revolution in Rushdie's mind.

3. See, for example, John Solomos' *Race and Racism in Britain* and Paul Gilroy's *There Ain't no Black in the Union Jack*, on the policies of the Conservative government towards immigrants from the so-called "new commonwealth" (India, the Caribbean, Africa) and Pakistan.

4. Stuart Hall has made a similar point to the one that Rushdie is making here, noting that, "...the term 'black' was coined as a way of referencing the common experience of racism and marginalization in Britain and came to provide the organizing category of a new politics of resistance, amongst groups and communities with, in fact, very different histories, traditions and ethnic identities. In this moment, politically speaking, 'The Black experience,' as a singular and unifying framework based on the building up of identity across ethnic and cultural difference between the different communities, became 'hegemonic' over other ethnic/racial identities—though the latter did not, of course, disappear" (Hall 252).

5. In *The Jaguar Smile*, Rushdie observes that "[t]he true purpose of masks, as any actor will tell you, is not concealment, but transformation. A culture of masks is one that understands a

good deal about the processes of metamorphosis" (*JS* 26). The transformation he writes of is the same as Bakhtin's notion of rebirth: the new subsuming the old.

6. Zeeny, Saladin's Indian lover, makes this racism explicit when she exclaims in exasperation at Saladin's blindspot: "They pay you to imitate them, as long as they don't have to look at you. Your voice becomes famous but they hide your face. Got any ideas why? Warts on your nose, cross-eyes, what? Anything come to mind, baby? You goddam lettuce brain, I swear" (*SV* 60).

WORKS CITED

Bakhtin, M.M. *Rabelais and his World*. Trans. Helene Iswolsky. Cambridge, Massachusetts: M.I.T. Press, 1968.

Bhabha, Homi. "Introduction: Locations of Culture." *The Location of Culture*. London: Routledge, 1994, 1-18.

____. "Representation and the Colonial Text: A Critical Exploration of Some Forms of Mimeticism." *The Theory of Reading*. Ed. Frank Gloversmith. Brighton: The Harvester Press, 1984, 93-122.

Gilroy, Paul. *There Ain't no Black in the Union Jack*. London: Hutchinson, 1987.

Hall, Stuart. "New Ethnicities." *'Race,' Culture & Difference*. Eds. James Donald and Ali Rattansi. London: SAGE, 1992, 252-59.

Harrison, James. *Salman Rushdie*. New York: Twayne, 1992.

Price Herndl, Diane. "The Dilemmas of a Feminine Dialogic." *Feminism, Bakhtin, and the Dialogic*. Ed. Dale M. Bauer and Susan Jaret McKinstry. New York: State U of New York P, 1991, 7-24.

Rushdie, Salman. *The Jaguar Smile: A Nicaraguan Journey*. London: Picador, 1987.

____. *The Satanic Verses*. London: Viking, 1988.

Russo, Mary. "Female Grotesques: Carnival and Theory." *Feminist Studies/Critical Studies*. Ed. Teresa de Lauretis. Bloomington: Indiana UP, 1986, 213-29.

Solomos, John. *Race and Racism in Britain*. 2nd ed. London: Macmillan, 1993.

Stallybrass, Peter and Allon White. *The Politics and Poetics of Transgression*. Ithaca, New York: Cornell UP, 1986.

Bibliography

Anon., "*Midnight's Children*—Memory's Recesses." *Northern India Patrika,* January 16, 1983.

Anon., "*Midnight's Children.*" *The Sunday Standard,* Book Review, June 14, 1981.

Appleyard, Bryan, "Portrait of the Novelist as a Hot Property." *The Sunday Times Magazine,* September 11, 1988.

Banerjee, Ashutosh, "Narrative Technique in *Midnight's Children.*" *Three Contemporary Novelists,* ed. R.K. Dhawan. New Delhi: Classical Publishing Co. 1985.

Batty, Nancy E., "The Art of Suspense: Rushdie's 1001 (Mid.) Night's." *Ariel,* Vol. 18, No. 3, July, 1987.

Bhattacharya, Soumya, "Exile on Main Street." *The Hindustan Times,* Lucknow edition, May 4, 2000.

Dharker, Rani, "An Interview with Salman Rushdie." *New Quest,* 42, Nov.-Dec., 1983.

Fernandez, Dileep, "Such Angst, Liveliness, Rootlessness." *Gentleman,* February, 1984.

Joshi, B.K., "It May Be Long But Its Not Overwritten." *The Times of India,* November 1, 1981.

Joshi, Rita, "Fantasy as Reality: The Art of Salman Rushdie." *The Sunday Observer,* April 12, 1987.

Mukerjee, Meenakshi, ed., *Midnight's Children: An Anthology of Recent Criticism.* New Delhi: Pencraft International, 1998.

Murti, V.K. Suryanarayan, "Secular Fantasy: Salman Rushdie's Fiction." *Kohinoor in the Crown: Critical Studies in Indian English Literature.* New Delhi: Sterling Publishers, 1987.

Naik, M.K., "A Life of Fragments: The Fate of Identity in *Midnight's Children.*" *Studies in Indian English Literature.* New Delhi: Sterling Publishers, 1987.

Narasimhaiah, C.D., "Spurious Reputations: Vikram Seth, Salman Rushdie and Shashi Tharoor." *Essays in Commonwealth Literature: Heirloom of Multiple Heritage.* Delhi: Pencraft International, 1995.

Pathak, R.S., "Rushdie on the Novel and Novelists." *Modern Indian Novel in English.* New Delhi: Creative Books, 1999.

Pathak, R.S., "History and the Individual in the Novels of Rushdie." *Three Contemporary Novelists,* ed. R.K. Dhawan, New Delhi: Classical Publishing Co., 1985.

Padgaonkar, Dileep, "Bambai Meri Jaan—A Conversation with Salman Rushdie." *The Times of India,* April 20, 2000.

Prasannarajan, S., "The Last Salaam." *Indian Express Magazine,* August 20, 1995.

Rao, K. Raghavendra, "The Novel as History as 'chutney:' Unriddling Salman Rushdie's *Midnight's Children.*" *Perspectives of Indian Fiction in English,* ed. M. Naik. New Delhi: Abhinav Publications, 1985.

Syal, P., "*Midnight's Children.*" *New Quest,* November-December, 1982.

——, "The Composite Structure of Rushdie's *Midnight's Children.*" *Structure and Style in Commonwealth Literature.* New Delhi: Vikas Publishing House Pvt. Ltd., 1993.

Verma, Charu, "Padma's Tragedy: A Feminist Deconstruction of *Midnight's Chidren.*" *Feminism and Recent Fiction in English,* ed. Sushila Singh. New Delhi: Prestige Publishers, 1991.

Wilson, Keith, "*Midnight's Children* and Reader's Responsibility." *The Critical Quarterly,* Vol. 26, No. 3, Autumn, 1984.

——, "Imaginary Truth that Brought Salman Rushdie Fame." *The Hindustan Times,* March 24, 1983.

Others

Anon., "Not Guilty!" *Sunday,* February 18-24, 1990.

——, "Raj Reversal" (Cover Story). *Sunday,* December 4-10, 1998.

——, "In Good Faith," *Sunday,* February—March 3, 1990.

——, Interview, *Northern India Patrika,* January 16, 1983.

——, Interview by Gordon Wise, *Gentleman,* February, 1984.

——, Interview, *The Sunday Observer,* September 6, 1987.

——, Interview, 'Network East,' BBC-2, September 24, 1988.

Contributors

Reena Mitra. Senior Reader, Department of English, Christ Church College, Kanpur, Uttar Pradesh.

Florence D'Souza. Lecturer in English, University of Lille 3, France.

Madan M. Sarma. Professor of English and Head, Department of English and Foreign Languages, Tezpur University, Tezpur, Assam.

Shyam S. Agarwalla. Principal, Dr. Ram Manohar Lohia College, Ranchi University, Ranchi, Bihar.

Ramesh Kumar Gupta. Department of English, Jai Prakash University, Chapra, Bihar.

Seema Bhaduri. Lecturer, Department of English, H.P.T. College, Nasik, Maharashtra.

Soumyajit Samanta. Department of English, Burdwan University, Burdwan, West Bengal.

Patrick Bixby. English Department, Emory University, No. 302 Callaway Center, 537 Kilgo Circle, Atlanta, GA 30322 USA.

Nandini Bhattacharya. Assistant Professor of English, Hooghly Mohsin College, Chinsurah, Hooghly, West Bengal.

Michael Hensen. University of Passau, Passau, Germany.

Blair Mahoney. Department of English and Cultural Studies, The University of Melbourne, Parkville, Victoria 3052, Australia.